"Rarely does a work of art like *Present Perfect* fall upon one's desk. This book allows us to transform existential pain caused by our need to be perfect. This book is abundant with tools and ideas that equip the reader to resolve guilt, shame, and perfectionism. Once you accept and surrender your perfectionism, the magical paradox of mindfulness as a healer will unfold."

—Ronald A. Alexander, Ph.D., executive director of the Open Mind Training Institute and author of *Wise Mind, Open Mind*

"Even those of us with a lot of self-help reading under our belts will experience many a-ha moments while immersed in *Present Perfect*. Somov's approach is highly logical, creative, resourceful, and compassionate. Never once will you feel judged; instead, you'll feel understood. I highly recommend this valuable resource to therapists and anyone with perfectionist tendencies."

—Dina Cheney, author of *Tasting Club* and Williams-Sonoma's *New Flavors for Salads*

"*Present Perfect* takes a wholly fresh look at an age-old problem by applying a generous dose of the healing salve of mindfulness. Filled with fascinating references and down-to-earth examples, this book skillfully guides the reader through exercises and strategies that can transform the paralyzing and demoralizing pattern of perfectionism. *Present Perfect* is the perfect way to liberate yourself from the guilt, shame, and blame of perfectionism and rediscover the freedom of living in the 'what is.'"

—Donald Altman, psychotherapist, former Buddhist monk, and author of *The Mindfulness Code*

"Pavel Somov offers an intelligent, witty, and compassionate critique of perfectionism and makes a compelling case that life is already perfect. I found this book to be thoroughly enjoyable and personally and professionally useful from the first page. I feel as comfortable recommending this book to my colleagues as I do to my patients and am confident that both will find it of tremendous value in their lives. Since perfectionism is often the other side of compulsive and addictive behavior, this book will be relevant to all who seek more moderation and balance in their lives."

—Andrew Tatarsky, Ph.D., clinical psychologist in New York City specializing in treating addictive behavior and author of *Harm Reduction Psychotherapy*

"This brilliant and practical new book is designed to help alleviate the excess stress and dissatisfaction of perfectionism, one of the main practices of the extremely popular, if unheralded, religion I lovingly call Control Freakism. Pavel Somov gives us numerous helpful awareness exercises, conscious inquiries, insights, mindfulness practices, original perspectives, and penetrating ideas, all conducive to helping us free ourselves from this tyrannical inner demon and experience the radiant reality of things just as they are. Acceptance has its own transformative magic, and I heartily recommend this work to all who want to transform, awaken, and edify."

—Lama Surya Das, founder of Dzogchen Meditation Centers and author of *Awakening the Buddha Within*

present
perfect

a mindfulness approach to
letting go of perfectionism
& the need for control

PAVEL SOMOV, PH.D.

New Harbinger Publications, Inc.

Publisher's Note

This publication is designed to provide accurate and authoritative informa-
tion in regard to the subject matter covered. It is sold with the understand-
ing that the publisher is not engaged in rendering psychological, financial,
legal, or other professional services. If expert assistance or counseling is
needed, the services of a competent professional should be sought.

Distributed in Canada by Raincoast Books

Copyright © 2010 by Pavel Somov
New Harbinger Publications, Inc.
5674 Shattuck Avenue
Oakland, CA 94609
www.newharbinger.com

FSC
Mixed Sources
Product group from well-managed
orests and other controlled sources

Cert no. SW-COC-002283
www.fsc.org
© 1996 Forest Stewardship Council

Acquired by Melissa Kirk; Cover design by Amy Shoup;
Edited by Carole Honeychurch; Text design by Michele Waters

Library of Congress Cataloging-in-Publication Data

Somov, Pavel G.
  Present perfect : a mindfulness approach to letting go of perfectionism
and the need for control / Pavel G. Somov.
       p. cm.
  Includes bibliographical references.
  ISBN 978-1-57224-756-7
  1. Perfectionism (Personality trait) 2. Control (Psychology) 3. Obsessive-
compulsive disorder. I. Title.
  BF698.35.P47S66 2010
  155.2'32--dc22
                        2010009353

12   11   10

10   9   8   7   6   5   4   3   2   1   First printing

To Thich Quang Duc*, who transcended the human ideal by accepting *what is*, one object of consciousness at a time, even while on fire.

* Thich Quang Duc, a sixty-six-year-old Buddhist monk, immolated himself on June 11, 1963, in protest of the persecution of Buddhists in South Vietnam. "As he burned, he never moved a muscle, never uttered a sound, his outward composure in sharp contrast to the wailing people around him" (Halberstam, 211).

contents

PART 1
introduction to perfectionism in general and to your
perfectionism in particular

CHAPTER 1

PART 2
perfectly imperfect, completely incomplete, and just so

CHAPTER 2

PART 3
overcoming mindlessness, guilt, shame, and motivational apathy

PART 4
rehabilitation of your self-view

introduction

In a sense, language is a museum of ignorance. Every word and concept has entered language at a stage of relative ignorance compared to our present greater experience. But the words and concepts are frozen into permanence by language, and we must use these words and concepts to deal with present-day reality. This means we may be forced to look at things in a very inadequate way.

—Edward de Bono

There seem to be three types of people on this planet: those who believe perfection is impossible, those who believe perfection is possible but is impossibly hard to attain, and those who think everything is already perfect. The latter group may consist primarily of those who are high, manic, or spiritually ecstatic. While, as a pragmatic realist, I don't share that sense of intoxication with life, I do agree with their conclusion.

Everything *is* perfect, all the time. Perfection—as I define it in this book—is not only attainable but inevitable. The goal of this book (to borrow from de Bono's imagery above) is to defrost this everyday/every-moment perfection that has been frozen up in the language of perfectionism and to satisfy your craving for perfection with a steady fix of the ordinary perfection that is all around us. In short, the goal of the book is to help you experience perfection without being perfectionistic.

introduction to perfectionism in general and to your perfectionism in particular

In this part you will learn about the symptoms of perfectionism, the motivations that underlie it, and its existential costs. You will also have an opportunity to get a jump-start on developing a mindfulness practice and will learn the seven goals of existential rehabilitation that will provide you with a general overview of the self-help journey ahead of you.

CHAPTER 1

360° of perfectionism

Once we become aware of what we are not, we begin to uncover and discover who and what we truly are... When we realize our true nature, we enter into the sphere of the luminous Great Perfection.

—Lama Surya Das

The body of your car is made of metal. The body of your perfectionism is made of mind (thoughts, feelings, and habits). Mind can change, and so can you! So roll up your self-help sleeves and jam the shovel of self-exploration into the ground of your being. Let's talk about perfectionism in general and your perfectionism in particular.

perfectionism: what it is and what it isn't

As a perfectionist, you like precision. In embarking on a self-help project, there's a good chance you want to know exactly what is wrong with you and what it's called. In my clinical practice, perfectionists tend to request diagnostic feedback more than other clients. This makes sense: information is power, and, as a perfectionist, you like to stay in control. So, without knowing anything about you in particular and extrapolating only from the fact that you're reading this book, here is my best diagnostic guess. You may be a bit OCPD (obsessive-compulsive *personality* disorder) but probably are not OCD (obsessive-compulsive disorder, a far more debilitating condition than OCPD; think Adrian Monk (Tony Shalhoub) in the television show *Monk*). Don't worry. You're in good company. In their authoritative book, *Perfectionism: Theory, Research, and Treatment*, Gordon Flett and Paul Hewitt note that "a strong case can be made for the claim that perfectionism is *endemic* to Western culture" (2002, xi). Even though OCPD may sound like a diagnostic handful, it's really just a way to describe a set of behaviors that can be seen as nearly normative for Western society. OCPD is just a framework to help you more clearly see the kinds of actions, attitudes, and thoughts that make someone a perfectionist.

Let me also throw this into the mix: chances are your prognosis is good. How can I assert that? Because perfectionists are a highly motivated lot, perfectly positioned for a self-help approach. My only lingering concern is for that type of perfectionist who tends to procrastinate, who might only skim through this book. If you think you're at risk for this, if you and I are meeting in passing, then I hope our minds will cross paths again, perhaps in a different book.

Getting back to the matter at hand: *perfectionism*, as the central feature of OCPD, is also characterized by such traits as excessive concern with details, an extreme devotion to work and productivity (at the expense of leisure), excessive conscientiousness, scrupulousness, thriftiness, inflexibility and rigidity in the issues of morality and ethics, reluctance to delegate tasks, and reluctance to relinquish control (Pfohl and Blum, 1991). However, what matters more than these symptoms is the motivation behind them, and we will get to that shortly.

In the meantime, let me note that perfectionism is mostly a result of learning, programming, and conditioning. I see it as an ingenious adaptation to a hypercritical, high-pressure, invalidating environment, a psychological self-defense strategy that unfortunately creates more problems than it solves. Most of the perfectionists I have worked with had perfectionistic or narcissistic (un-empathic and invalidating) parents. Aside from parental influence, the extent of perfectionism depends on the culture you live in. Some societies are more culturally perfectionistic than others. The so-called "developed societies," for example, tend to emphasize "efficiency, punctuality, a willingness to work hard, and orientation to detail." Of course, these are the very traits that may accompany perfectionism and OCPD (Millon and Davis, 2000, 174).

Perfectionism can be directed at oneself and/or at others (Flett and Hewitt, 2002). *Self-directed* (inwardly oriented) perfectionists are notoriously hard on themselves: if they make a mistake, they shred themselves to pieces in ruminating bouts of merciless self-scrutiny. While self-directed perfectionists are their own worst critics, *other-directed* (outwardly focused) perfectionists are tough on others and are easily frustrated by others' imperfections.

The literature on perfectionism also distinguishes between *generalized* (or "extreme") perfectionism (in which perfectionists pursue "extreme standards across a variety of life domains") and *situational* perfectionism (in which perfectionism is limited to specific areas of life) (Flett and Hewitt, 2002, 16). Situational perfectionism is, up to a point, adaptive and useful. Indeed, some jobs have extremely narrow margins of error and require great attention to detail (for instance, surgeon, air traffic controller, accountant). However, when perfectionism becomes a way of living (rather than a way of earning a living), then you have a case of generalized or extreme perfectionism.

the existential costs of perfectionism

On January 6, 2009, CNN reported that German billionaire Adolf Merckle died by suicide, jumping in front of a train because his fortunes had declined from $12.8 billion to $9.2 billion in 2008. CNN offered the following explanation: "The financial troubles of his companies, induced by the international financial crisis and the uncertainty and powerlessness to act independently…broke the passionate family business man, and he took his own life" (CNN, 2009). My clinical guess is that Adolf Merckle was a casualty of perfectionism, not of the economy. CNN's explanation of the reasons behind the suicide is replete with red flags of perfectionism. Let's take a close look at this psychological autopsy. The press release notes that the suicide was precipitated by the "financial troubles" of Merckle's companies. Merckle didn't lose everything; he didn't go broke—he just moved down in rank from forty-fourth to ninety-fourth on the Forbes list of the world's richest people. His fortunes "declined," but they didn't vanish. This was a case of partial failure, not complete failure. But, for the all-or-nothing perfectionistic mind, partial failure means total failure. The press release indicates that Merckle was troubled by "uncertainty and powerlessness to act independently." This is typical of perfectionists, as they are indeed threatened by the prospect of relinquishing control. Merckle, according to this press release, was a "passionate family business man." The significance that I see here has to do with the typical blurring of private and professional. Merckle's business was a family business, therefore professional failures were personal failures. But even if his business had not been a family business, Merckle, if he was at all like other perfectionists I know, would have probably taken his professional failings personally. That's what perfectionists do: they live for success and depend on it for meaning.

Vincent Foster, the former Deputy White House Counsel under President Clinton, died by suicide and is another likely casualty of perfectionism. In an article on the destructiveness of perfectionism, Yale psychiatrist Sidney Blatt wrote that Foster was "typical of numerous examples of talented, ambitious, and successful individuals who are driven by intense needs for perfection and plagued by intense self-scrutiny, self-doubt, and self-criticism" (1995, 1005).

Let's face it: perfectionism isn't cheap. In fact, perfectionism is existentially unaffordable, as it exacts a high psychological price of anxiety, worry, and depression (Maxmen and Ward, 1995). Perfectionists are "more likely than nonperfectionists to experience various kinds of stress" (Flett and Hewitt, 2002, 257). If unaddressed, perfectionism is a serious relational liability that can lead to alienation and missed social opportunities. Many perfectionists are pushed into therapy by family and friends to address the problems of anger and hypercriticism and to work on their control tendencies and their insistence on being right. Perfectionism can also lower your productivity. Perfectionistic preoccupation with outcome distracts the mind from the actual work process and creates performance anxiety that, in turn, undermines productivity or leads to procrastination. Similarly, perfectionism can stand in the way of your creativity. Perfectionists like to play it safe, stick to the protocol, and not take chances in order to avoid mistakes. This kind of emphasis on consistency is a wet blanket on any creative spark of experimentation and spontaneity. Moral or ethical perfectionism can result in a spiritual crisis and lead to a deficit of kindness and compassion. Perfectionism costs money, time, and resources. Perfectionists might be prone to fix what isn't quite broken, to redo entire projects because of minor perceived imperfections and flaws. While perfectionism offers the short-lived reassurance of structure from the ambiguity and uncertainty of life, ultimately it constrains your choices and sense of freedom. In sum, perfectionism is an existential trap.

your particular perfectionism

There are different forms of perfectionism, and you may have a tendency toward one or another. We'll examine these different manifestations more closely later in the book. For now, the following several exercises can help you get started in making sense of your perfectionism. You don't have to do all of these exercises in one sitting. Pick a couple to journal about. Read through the rest and come back to them when you have time. However, I do suggest that you work through each and every exercise in the book no matter how obvious or odd it might seem at a glance. Each exercise sets an experiential precedent: it lays the tracks of memory in your mind for a similar train of thought to run on later. As a final note on exercises, I'd like to point out that the exercises are sometimes strategically placed to orchestrate a particular build-up of a target experience. Whenever that is the case, I will cue you to pause to engage in a given exercise before you read on. Most of the time, however, I will simply include one or more exercises to go along with a given point.

Exercise: Why Are You Reading this Book?

What prompted you to invest your time in this book? Did you have an epiphany about your life and its impact on others? Did somebody give you this book to read? How did you react to their suggestion? What do you want to change in your life as a result of reading this book? Document your thoughts in your journal.

Exercise: What's the History of Your Perfectionism?

Who do you think "programmed" you to aspire to be perfect? Who loved you so conditionally that they needed you to be perfect? Who was so perfectionistic with you that you had to be perfect to be accepted and loved? Whose margin of error was so unforgiving that just being you wasn't enough? For whose attention, love, and approval were you competing? Note any particular phrases or slogans from your upbringing that got stuck in your mind (maybe something like "Failure is not an option!").

Exercise: What Are the Costs of Your Perfectionism?

What's been the cost of your perfectionism? Anxiety, worry, depression? Failed relationships? Procrastination? What passed you by as you crossed the t's and dotted the i's?

Exercise: How Do You See the Cost of Imperfection?

What does your imperfection say about you as a person? What are the costs of being imperfect? What threatens you about being less than perfect? Document your thoughts.

Exercise: Do You Know Anyone Who Is Perfect?

Do you know anyone perfect? What makes them perfect? Are they perfect in absolutely every respect? If not, then are they still perfect? If you don't know anyone who is totally perfect, then what do you make of your own pursuit of perfection? With whom are you competing? God? Journal on this.

Exercise: What Are Your Imperfections?

Catalog your imperfections. Make a list of your life's biggest mistakes and ponder the extent to which these mistakes were a function of imperfections or a function of your perfectionism.

Exercise: How Are You Programming Your Children?

This one is only for the parents. Are you expecting your children to be perfect? If so, why? If not, why not? Why the double standard? Are you trying to spare them the turmoil of perfectionism? If so, how do you plan to model self-acceptance to your children when you are so unforgiving of yourself? Wrestle with this one.

Exercise: How Do You Define Perfection?

Imagine that you are defining the idea of perfection for a dictionary. Go beyond the specifics. "Perfection is..." Fill in the blank.

understanding the motivation behind perfectionism

In making sense of perfectionism, I distinguish between primary and secondary perfectionism.

Primary perfectionism is a pursuit of perfection for its own sake, as an end in and of itself. Primary perfectionism is when you want reality to be better than it is because you think it could be or should be better. (In principle, there's nothing wrong with striving for a better world. It's just that in practice, constant striving for a better world obscures the ordinary perfection of the world that already is.)

In *secondary perfectionism*, trying to be perfect is a means to an end, and the pursuit of perfection is secondary to the psychological, relational, and existential dividends of being perfect (more about this below).

Perfectionism Is a Striving on a Feedback Loop

Perfectionism is akin to an insatiable appetite: no matter how much you have, it's never enough. Buddhist psychology posits that the cause of suffering is an unremitting striving for more and offers a useful metaphor of a hungry ghost (*preta* in Sanskrit). Pretas are portrayed with bloated stomachs and necks as narrow as a needle's eye, so that food cannot pass fast enough to satisfy their desires. Just like perfectionists, pretas are perpetually dissatisfied: the more they want, the emptier they feel. That's the thing about incessant striving: it empties us out. Say you are content with what you have, and you don't want anything else. You are full. Then you see something that you want. So you think that if you could only have what you want, you'd be even fuller and life would be even better—it would be perfect. If you allow this desire to grow into an obsession, soon you'll feel that what you already have isn't enough. The desire leads to a loss of contentment. What happens next is a runaway feedback loop of dissatisfaction: the more you want something that you don't have, the less you are content with what you do have; the less you are content with what you have, the more you want that which you don't have. And so it goes, round and round, until you find yourself in a knot of suffering.

Three Types of Perfectionistic Hunger

In striving for perfection, what have you been actually craving? As I see it, there are three types of perfectionistic hunger: approval/validation hunger, reflection/attention hunger, and control/certainty hunger.

Approval/Validation-Hunger Perfectionism

A pat on the back, a word of praise, or a nod of approval can sure feel validating and can put a self-doubting mind at ease. Approval-hungry/validation-hungry perfectionism parallels the so-called *conscientious compulsive* variant of OCPD (Millon and Davis 2000). Conscientious compulsives tend to be hard working, dutiful, and ever eager to meet others' expectations. They fear "that failure to perform perfectly will lead to both abandonment and condemnation" by others (2000, 176). This makes sense: when you're perfect, people generally like you (unless they are threatened by your perfection), and they come to depend on you. As a result, you feel valuable and indispensable. The downside, of course, is that you have to constantly strive to meet everyone's expectations and you essentially live in fear of others' disapproval of you.

Reflection/Attention-Hunger Perfectionism

At a certain stage of our growing up it is essential that we feel seen, acknowledged, and attended to. This is known in psychological terms as being *mirrored*. Perfectionism can be an adaptation to a deficit of mirroring. Growing up with an insecure, possibly narcissistic parent, you might have lost your sense of self because you were compelled to serve as a mirror for your parent's hungry ego. And now the only way for you to feel good about yourself is to stand out by being perfect. Some reflection-hungry perfectionists seek out attention; others demand it, commanding special treatment and insisting on unquestioning compliance with their wishes, both trying to be perfect themselves and demanding nothing less than perfection from others. If you recognize yourself in this, cut yourself some slack: you aren't bad, you're just starved.

Control/Certainty-Hunger Perfectionism

Life is confusing and full of the unexpected. It tests our predictive acumen and frustrates our assumptions. So, in order to go on and not surrender to the chaos of life, we crave certainty, we yearn for a sense of control, we seek reassurance that we are on the right track. To deal with this uncertainty and lack of control, we shop around for a philosophy of living, for some kind of ideological structure or guidance. Once we find something that makes half-decent sense, we latch on to it. As we become invested in a particular way of living and thinking, we become understandably threatened by differences. Ideas different from our own make us second-guess our own approach to life, undermining our hard-earned sense of certainty and control. Some of us respond by becoming more rigid. We might even fight back by insisting that others should live, think, and act the way we do. So, in trying to protect our sense of control, we become judgmental and controlling. This kind of principled perfectionism is common in the area of ethics and morality, and it runs a close parallel to the so-called *puritanical compulsive* variant of OCPD, which is characterized by being uncompromising and dogmatic (Millon and Davis 2000).

Though you may not like the sound of it, you should recognize that hunger for control and certainty (just like hunger for approval, validation, reflection, and attention) is a normal part of who we are. We all start out as a bit needy and afraid. We are all new to this bewildering world. Living, like any skill, has a learning curve to it. If you're reading this, you are climbing that curve.

Exercise: What's Eating Me?

Ask yourself: What am I hungering for? What am I chasing—perfection, approval, certainty, validation? Why am I seeking all this? How am I incomplete without it all? What's amiss? Do I really need what I'm chasing, or do I just want it? What will approval prove? What will validation validate? What will certainty protect me from?

Ask yourself: Whose stamp of approval am I striving for and why? Whose pat on my back has the power of the Midas touch that makes me feel golden, valuable, worthwhile? Whose opinion of me do I worship, seek out, cater to? Who has the power and wisdom to reassure me of all my fears and insecurities? Whose validation, attention, and acknowledgment do I need in order to feel visible and justified in my existence?

Then ask yourself: Who promoted this person/these people to this special status? How did they earn such clout, such influence in my life? How have I gotten by all these years without that which I'm still chasing?

Feeding the Hungry Ghost of Perfectionism

So, if perfectionism is metaphorical hunger (for approval/validation, reflection/attention, or control/certainty), then how can we satisfy it? With the bread of acceptance. Borrowing language from Buddhist psychology, I offer you the following treatment ("feeding") plan:

1. The experience of reality as imperfect (dissatisfaction with reality the way it is) exists and is inevitable.

2. The source of this suffering/dissatisfaction is a desire or an expectation for reality to be different from how it is,

to be better than it is. In other words, the source of perfectionistic suffering is the striving to perfect *what is*.

3. Perfectionism can be cured through the acceptance of reality for what it is *in its perfectly imperfect suchness*. (I'll explain more about the notion of "suchness" in a bit.)

How's this acceptance achieved? The short answer is: through mindfulness (the technique) and mindful living (as a consciously chosen philosophy of living). To get the long answer, read the rest of this book.

the staff of mindfulness

Mindfulness, as a philosophy of living, is a pledge of allegiance to the present, a commitment to not only the destination of your journey but also "being there" every step of the way. As a technique, mindfulness is a tool to support yourself on this journey of life.

Long, long before smart phones, a walking stick was our support staff when on the go. A good walking staff was the ultimate assistive device. If you misstepped, the staff helped you regain your balance. If you tired, the staff was there to support you. The staff offered the benefit of a probe if you needed to explore an unfamiliar object along the way. It could be used as a gauge to test the depth of water if you had to ford a stream. If you needed to commit something to memory, you could notch the information down on the staff more or less with the same ease as we do it with the flash-drive memory sticks of today. And if necessary, a staff could be readily used as a weapon. All in all, the staff helped clear the way of obstacles.

Whereas acceptance of the ordinary perfection of *what is* is the destination of our walk in this book, mindfulness—metaphorically speaking—will be your walking staff. As an assistive psychological device, mindfulness will help you traverse the turbulent streams of your consciousness. It will prop you up when you stumble over some imperfection, help you remember what you are and what you are not, and clear away the debris of illusions on your way to well-being.

I believe the entire human civilization as we know it began with mindfulness. First, living in the jungle of life, we were too busy surviving to sit down. When we finally figured out how to use fire to protect us, we got a chance to relax. When we sat down in a circle around the first fire, for the first time in the history of our species with nothing to do, we noticed ourselves. We noticed the fire dance of our mortal impermanence and the circular interdependence of us all. This was our first *zazen*, our first sitting meditation, our first species-wide experience of mindfulness, the dawn of self-awareness. Some of us were immediately spooked by the realization of our impermanence and interdependence and reacted by psychologically separating from this realization. This separation, these I–you, me–it, self–other, subject–object, mind–body, man–nature distinctions, led to dualism. As soon as we separated ourselves from reality, we started trying to control it, improve it, and perfect it. Having inevitably failed, instead of accepting our limitations, we chose to transcend them. We started to strive. *Perfectionism was born*. While we ran from ourselves and our deeper connections, there were always others who stayed seated, transfixed and inspired by the fire dance of impermanence. It is from these "babysitters" (monks, mystics, meditators, introspectors, hermits, and inner-nauts) of our primordial consciousness that we all have been trying to re-learn how to be a human *being*, not a human *doing*.

As a special kind of awareness, mindfulness involves two essential mechanisms: 1) *passive attention* and 2) *dis-identification*. Attention can be active or passive, that of an active observer or that of an uninvolved witness. This distinction is easy to understand through the contrast of such verbs as "to look" and "to see." "To look" implies an active visual scanning, a kind of goal-oriented visual activity. "To see" implies nothing other than a fact of visual registration. Let's say I lost my house keys. I would have to look for them. But in the process of looking for my house keys, I might also happen to see an old concert ticket. Mindfulness is about seeing, not looking. It is about "just" noticing and "just" witnessing without an attachment to or identification with what is being noticed and witnessed. But how do you *do* this mindfulness thing? By *not doing* it. James Austin, a professor emeritus of neurology and the author of *Zen and the Brain*, puts it this way: "It is a letting go of oneself, of letting things happen, of *not* striving. This means *not trying* to do something. It also means not trying *not* to do something. Finally, a state beyond trying arrives" (1999, 142). "A state beyond trying"— a state beyond striving, beyond craving, beyond seeking, beyond reaching—is a state beyond perfectionism.

Exercise: Watching the River (the "Dots" Exercise)

James Austin, the author and neurologist I mentioned earlier, called this state of effortless witnessing a "riverbank attitude."

Watch your thoughts. Each and every time you recognize that you have a new thought event (mental image, sensation, feeling), mark down a dot on a piece of paper with a pen or a pencil. Set an alarm clock for five minutes and watch your mind like this while marking down dots, one after another. Remain a dispassionate observer of whatever pops into your head, as if you were sitting on the bank of a river watching boats pass by. Just watch the mind flow, the thoughts come and pass down the river, staying where you are, in this riverbank attitude, without getting carried away downriver and without getting caught up in any thought. When the time is up, look at the dots on the paper. Realize that the thoughts came and went, but you're still here. Tip: This exercise is meant to be an opportunity for you to learn how to step back from what you think, feel, or sense. This exercise is designed to help you begin to tune in to what you are by recognizing what you are not. You are not your thoughts.

Practice this exercise daily as you "walk" your way through this book. Mindfulness will serve as an invaluable walking staff on your journey to acceptance.

Exercise: The Dots and Spaces

Building on the preceding exercise, let's add an element of breath focus to leverage the calming effect of this meditation. Once again, you'll need a pen/pencil, a piece of paper, and your lungs. Begin by paying attention to the breath. Simply notice your breath as it is. And as soon as you are distracted by a thought or some other sensation, put down a dot on the piece of paper.

As soon as you put down a dot, return to the awareness of your breath. Keep at it for a few minutes. Go ahead and try this now, before you read on.

Good. Now, look at the paper. Recognize that the dots correspond to mental events, to mind events. Each dot was some kind of thought, some kind of informational event, an object of consciousness, a slice of the mindstream. Now, what about the spaces in between the dots? What do you think the spaces could stand for? These fleeting moments of emptiness, these spaces between the thoughts, these moments of pure awareness, these moments of informationally untainted presence—that is you. You are not your thoughts, sensations, or feelings. After all, they come and go. You are what remains. These mind events (thoughts, feelings, sensations) are, indeed, a part of you but no more than a reflection is a part of the mirror. You are the space in between these mind dots, the consciousness from which these thoughts emerge, the consciousness into which these thoughts dissolve. Now try this exercise again. Settle into the space that you are. Take a note of this sense of unqualified and indescribable presence: here you are, the real you, the one that doesn't change, the one that is beyond evaluation and comparison; simply here, not going anywhere, invulnerable and unafraid. It's nothing special. And that's what makes it permanent.

Exercise: Watching the River (Portable Version)

This is a more portable version of the river-watching meditation: instead of jotting down dots, rest one of your hands with its palm down on top of your knee and gently tap away the thoughts with your index finger. So, each and every time you witness your mind change, each and every time you notice a new thought, feeling, or sensation arrive onto the shores of your awareness, tap it away.

You might be curious about this whole business of jotting down dots or taps. This is something I've stumbled upon in my own practice and used as a meditation teaching method. Here's how I see it: each thought is the beginning of an action sequence. In a manner of speaking, each thought wants to be born, it wants to graduate to a level of action. It carries an action/impulse potential. The tap (or the jotting down) discharges this action potential, grounding the energy in a generic, nonspecific manner, thus completing the "life cycle" of a thought. The tap (or the dot) is a behavioral deflection. In my own meditation practice, in discussing mediation with others, and in sharing it with my clients, I have long noticed a pattern of people sud-

denly bolting out of meditation. So, here you sit, watching your mind, and most of the time you do just fine. But now and then something emotionally charged sneaks up on you, gets to you—and you bolt. I've found that this jotting/tapping element serves as an effective way to bolt without bolting, to act out without abandoning the meditation place. The added benefit of using the tap rather than jotting down dots is that you can use this exercise on the go.

Exercise: Sneak Meditation into Real Life

People tap their fingers (particularly when stressed or impatient) all the time. Try the river-watching exercise with the finger tap during a real-life situation. Say you're at a difficult, emotionally charged business meeting. You don't like what's going on. You've got some nasty thought in a pre-launch state of readiness on the tip of your tongue. No, you're not losing it exactly, but you are about to say something that you might regret (or worry about later on). With one of your hands (palm down) on your knee, practice mentally stepping back from what's going on. Notice the thoughts, feelings, and sensations that are flooding you and gently, inconspicuously, tap them away.

Exercise: Just Sit and Watch

After a couple of weeks of practicing the meditations above, try either the river-watching or the river-watching-plus-breath-focus meditation without either jotting down or tapping away the thoughts. Just sit and watch the mind flow. There's nothing to do, nowhere to go. You made time to be here, so be here. The world will wait. Remember that the whole business of jotting dots or tapping away thoughts is just a set of training wheels on a bicycle. When you've learned to stay balanced and unperturbed by the passing thoughts, you can go for a ride without these assistive devices.

Exercise: Watch Your Perfectionism Pass

As I mentioned at the beginning of the chapter, your entire perfectionism is made of mind (thoughts, feelings, habits, and defenses). Mind constantly changes: thoughts come and go, feelings ebb and flow. I'd like for you to watch your perfectionism. Think of some mistake that you made. Get close to it. Recall the details. And as soon as this process of recalling-on-demand begins to acquire the free-flowing nature of dwelling, kick back and watch the flow of your perfectionistic rumination. Watch it the same way you channel-surf TV. If it fails to hold your attention, make a conscious choice to change the channel and move on.

conclusion: seven elements of existential rehabilitation

The following are the seven habits that, in my opinion, compose the basis of existentially vibrant living and appear to be in particular deficit in the life of a perfectionist:

1. The habit of making your own meaning

2. The habit of noticing ordinary perfection

3. The habit of being present in the moment

4. The habit of making conscious choices

5. The habit of self-acceptance

6. The habit of accepting uncertainty

7. The habit of forgiving and compassion

These seven vital signs of conscious, meaningful, and mindful living are the goals of the program of existential rehabilitation laid out in this book. I predict that developing these habits will help you feel freer and more alive, more at ease and invulnerable, more attuned to yourself and more connected with others, and, most importantly, less preoccupied with what should be and more in awe of what already is.

PART 2

perfectly imperfect, completely incomplete, and just so

This part is of interest to all types of perfectionists. It offers the essential framework for the rest of the book.

broadening the meaning of perfection

One truth is clear, Whatever is, is right.

—Alexander Pope

Goodness and being are really the same...[E]verything is perfect so far as it is actual. Therefore it is clear that a thing is perfect so far as it exists.

—St. Thomas Aquinas

If the introduction was a handshake and chapter 1 was a sales pitch, chapter 2 is where I begin to explain the key feature of the "widget" you've bought—that of *acceptance of reality as it is*. My goal in this chapter is to redefine perfection in a manner that will enable you to recognize perfection without being perfectionistic.

Before you read on, I want to give you a heads-up. The house of perfectionism sits on a flimsy logical foundation. As I begin to bulldoze this perfectionistic slum castle in the sky down to the ground of reality, you might find yourself bristling a bit. This is entirely normal. Upon hearing my argument, every perfectionist I have worked with has first mounted a passionate counteroffensive but has eventually come around to see the logic of this new perspective on perfection. When you're done reading through this chapter, you will have a choice of how to view perfection. The fate of your perfectionism depends on which view you choose. If you decide to keep your original view of perfection, your perfectionism will live another day. If you accept the new view of perfection offered in this chapter, you will take one hell of a wrecking ball to the prison of perfectionism.

the warm-up

Let me throw a couple of curveballs at you as a warm-up, and then we'll take it one step at a time. Imagination is always at least one step ahead of reality. When we appraise the world, ourselves, or others, we compare what is (the real) with what theoretically could be (the imagined). Say you got a B on a test. You look at this grade and you think that you could have done better, that you could have gotten an A. But that's theory. The reality is that you got a B, not an A, and this B represented your practical (not theoretical) best. With this in mind, let me ask you this: What do you mean by perfection— the theoretical best or the practical best? When you think about perfection, are you thinking about the imaginary perfection of what could be or about the perfection of what actually is? Of course, this is something of a rhetorical question. I know the answer: as a perfectionist, you define perfection as a theoretical best. That's exactly why you are never satisfied with reality as it is. The real world—the one and only world that there is at any given point in time—always pales in comparison with a better world that you can imagine. In any comparison of the real and the ideal, the ideal, by definition, comes out on top and the real loses out. No matter how great you are, you can always imagine yourself being even better. This conclusion is in the nature of imagination: fiction is always one step ahead of fact. The tragedy of perfectionism is that a comparison of what is with what could be is a foregone conclusion. To repeat: the ideal, the fictional, the imaginary is always better than the real, the factual, the existent. Thus, perfectionism is a destiny of dissatisfaction.

Here's another curveball: what is more valuable—a real twenty-dollar bill or an imaginary one-hundred-dollar bill? Once again, I'm being rhetorical. I'm sure you'd say that a real twenty-dollar bill is more valuable than an imaginary one-hundred-dollar bill (and if I'm wrong, feel free to mail me a check for twenty dollars and I will reciprocate with a fake one-hundred-dollar bill). But if that is so, then how do you end up concluding that the perfection of what is (the real, practical best) ends up being less valuable than the imaginary perfection of what could be? How does an actual B on the test become less valuable than an imaginary A? How does an actual moment of performance in your life seem less valuable to you than an imaginary moment of performance that never took place? Once again, I am being rhetorical *and* so are you, by the way, if you're thinking that the B you got on the test could have been an A. Rhetorically (theoretically), it could have been. In practice, however, it couldn't have been. Sure, you can get an A in the future; that remains an option. But if you *could* have gotten a B instead of an A on a given test, then you *would* have gotten an A, not a B. To continue to believe that what happened didn't have to happen and what didn't happen should have happened is to believe in a fictional history of an actual fact. Okay—enough with the curveballs for now. Let's roll out the idea of acceptance of what is one step at a time.

problem: rejection of what is

As a perfectionist, you reject reality. It's just not good enough for you. Otherwise, why would you be trying to perfect it? You feel this reality could be better than it is. That's why you are striving to perfect *what is* to be in line with how you think this reality *should be*. That's optimistic of you. But optimism, just like pessimism, isn't realism. Moreover, your optimistic expectation inevitably leads to a pessimistic conclusion: the real is always worse than the ideal.

solution: acceptance of what is

To overcome perfectionism, you'd have to learn to accept reality for what it is at any given moment. I can imagine the objections: "What? Accept the reality as it is? You must be kidding me!" Not at all. There are two reasons to accept reality as it is. First, there is no other reality at any given point in time than the one that there is. We can think of things being different from how they are at this point in time, but this hypothetically better, ideal reality exists only in our minds. In reality, there is just reality. So, what else is there to accept but this? The second reason for accepting the present reality as it is? It's already perfect.

extending the meaning of perfection

As a problem, perfectionism begins with an unnecessarily narrow understanding of the notion of perfection itself. Typically, we see perfection as an ideal state of affairs, a state of immaculate flaw-lessness, a state that is error-free, so complete that nothing can be added to it to make it better. Perfection, then, is *a state that is beyond improvement*. When we think of a state that is beyond betterment, we tend to think of it as the best that can theoretically be. Therefore, we equate perfection with theoretical excellence.

But here's a curious paradox. If perfection is a state beyond improvement, then isn't every moment, by definition, perfect? After all, any given "now," any given moment of reality is what it is in the sense that it cannot be anything other than what it is. Take *this* moment, *right now*: this moment is already here, and, as such, as theoretically imperfect as it may be, it is—at present—beyond any modification. While you could take the lessons of this moment and try to make the next moment better, this very moment is beyond improvement. It is too late to add anything to this moment to make it better. And if this moment, this slice of reality, is beyond improvement, then it's the only way it can be (the best it can be—perfect).

Present = Perfect

Any moment—by virtue of its already being present—is beyond betterment and is therefore perfect. From this point on, when you think of perfection, think of the present. And when you think of the present, think of perfection. After all, what is present *is* perfect! Perfection exists in reality, not in theory. Sure, we can think of perfection only as some theoretical state of excellence. That is certainly useful. Envisioning a better reality is pivotal to goal setting and progress. But why limit ourselves to just that? Why not also begin to notice the ordinary perfection of what is? Why not extend our definition of perfection to include the ordinary perfection of what is? Perfection isn't just what could be—perfection is also what is. Perfection isn't only theory—perfection is also reality. This is so not because reality matches theory but because any given slice of reality is beyond improvement and is, therefore, the best that it can be right now. Why strive for perfection only to ignore it?

Perfect = Completed = Complete

The word "perfect" comes to us from the Old French *parfit*, which in turn stems from the Latin *perfectus*, which means "completed" (Online Etymology Dictionary, s.v. "perfect"). If you consult a Latin–English dictionary for the word *perfectus* you will get "complete, finished, done/perfect, without flaw" (note the order of these meanings). JM Latin-English dictionary translates the verb *perficio* as to "complete, finish, execute, bring about, accomplish, do thoroughly" (once again, note the order of meanings). Thinking of the word "perfect" in the connotation of "completed" rather than "complete" makes good sense. What's completed *is* complete. What has occurred, what has taken place, is already a fact. It can't be made into anything more than it is. One cannot add to a fact. A fact—just like perfection—is beyond improvement.

Follow the logic of this new meaning of perfection:

1. If it (whatever "it" might be) is, it has happened.

2. If it has happened, it has been completed.

3. If it has been completed, it is complete.

4. If it is complete, there is nothing to add to it to make it better.

5. If there is nothing to add to it to make it better, it is as good as it can be right now.

6. If it is as good as it can be right now, it is beyond improvement.

7. If it is beyond improvement, then how isn't it perfect?

8. If it is the only way it can be right now, then how isn't it the right way?

A Perfectionist Pursues Perfection, a Realist Perceives It

To a perfectionist, reality is always imperfect because one can always imagine something better. To a nonperfectionist, the present reality is either 1) perfect (because it's the best it can be at the moment) or 2) neither perfect nor imperfect; it is what it is. A realist accepts the present as it is and rolls with it to improve the next moment. A perfectionist rejects the present as not being good enough and gets stuck in a state of perfectionistic dissatisfaction. A perfectionist compares what is with what could be, the real with the ideal, and pursues the imaginary perfection. On the contrary, a realist sees the present as complete and therefore perceives the actual perfection of what is. To a perfectionist, *the present is absence* of what could be and a reason to hurry up to improve the reality of what is. To a realist, *the present is presence* of all that can be and an opportunity to be mindfully and patiently present with what is.

acceptance is courage, not surrender

Acceptance isn't passivity or surrender. It's an active engagement in reality, in real time, on its terms. As such, acceptance is realism and requires existential courage rather than an escapist flight into what theoretically could be. Accepting reality as it is now means just that: accepting the reality as it is *right now*. If you don't like the way reality is right now, change the future. You see, acceptance isn't approval, it's just an acknowledgment of what is (more about this below). If you don't acknowledge what is, what will you be improving?

You might think: If I am to accept that at any given time I am as perfect as I can be at that moment, then how am I to achieve my goals? How am I to improve myself? The false choice here is this: *either* accept *or* change. Acceptance of the fact that at any given time you're doing your practical best (however unsatisfying it might be to you or others) doesn't mean that you can't try to improve the next moment. Of course you can. Accept *and* change: accept that at any given moment you are doing the best you can do *and*, having learned from the experience of this given moment, try to change and improve the next moment to the extent that you can. Automatic, on-the-fly perfectionistic rejection of reality as flawed triggers a mindless rush to improve it. Acceptance, beginning with the acknowledgment of what is as being the best that it can be, is the beginning of mindful change.

Exercise: What Is My New Definition of Perfection?

Review your original definition of perfection (see exercise in chapter 1). How do you see perfection now? What are the implications of this new definition of perfection, of this new way of looking at yourself, others, and the world at large? Contrast your answers with your previous essay on the meaning of perfection (from chapter 1).

Exercise: Reality Check vs. Theory Check

Get two lined index cards. On the first card, write down the following ideas. "He/she is doing the best that he/she can." "If reality could be different right now, it would be—this is the only reality that there is right now. This is all there is." "Just because reality (or this particular situation) could be better at a different point in time and under different circumstances, that doesn't mean that it can be different right now. If it could be different right now, then this situation wouldn't be this situation, it would be a different situation." This will be your reality-check/reality-acceptance card.

On the second card, write down the following ideas. "This reality (situation) could be so much better." "I could be doing so much better right now than I'm doing. I'm shortchanging myself." "I have a potential to do better, but I'm not using it because I'm not doing as well as I could in theory." "He/she could be doing so much better than he/she is doing." "This is unacceptable because it's not ideal." "This shouldn't be the way it is." "This should not have happened. This should have been prevented because, in theory, it could have been prevented." This will be your theory-check/reality-rejection card.

In the next week, whenever you find yourself frustrated with reality or yourself, pull out both cards, read through them, and select the statement that feels the best. After a week, tear up the card that seems to be of least value in helping you cope.

Say something happens that you didn't expect. A classic perfectionistic thought pops into your mind: "This wasn't supposed to happen!" You didn't suppose it would, but it did. Who's wrong here: reality or your theory about reality?

You see, we constantly match our ambitious minds against the bewildering complexity of reality, testing our assumptions, suppositions, hypotheses, and theories. As a perfectionist, when you find yourself in a situation where the reality doesn't match your theory, you conclude that it is the reality that is wrong, not your theory. But reality is never wrong. As Alexander Pope astutely observed, "Whatever is, is right" (2006). So here's a humility check for you to try.

Exercise: Humility Check

Whenever something goes "wrong" (meaning not the way you supposed it would go), choose to shift from frustration to awe. Marvel at the bewildering, nuanced, multifaceted complexity of what is. Say to yourself, "Wow!" Instead of chastising yourself, allow that you made the best prediction you could about how reality would be, but you have obviously and understandably underestimated the mind-boggling complexity of it all. Perhaps you weren't aware of all the variables involved; maybe you didn't have enough computational sophistication to extrapolate the most likely trajectory of reality. How could have you known what you didn't know? If you had known what you didn't know, your predictions would have been different. It's time to factor in the new data, to update your assumptions, to revise your model, and to say "Wow!" (not "Damn!").

Exercise: New Mind Order

To reprogram your view of perfection, write down each of the statements below and make it a point to review them a few times a day for a few days until each idea sinks in.

- It is what it is.

- Perfectly imperfect; completely incomplete.

- Stop trying to remodel reality—live in it!

- A perfectionist pursues perfection—a realist perceives it.

- There is no parallel reality that is just like this one but better.

- If it could be better, then it would be better.

- Accept the present. Change the future.

- ■ The present is already perfect: perfect the future.

- ■ Shoulda, coulda, woulda, buddha (with the lowercase word "buddha" here meaning "acceptance of what is").

A *holodeck* is a simulated reality facility (in the *Star Trek: The Next Generation* TV series) used for recreation and tactical training. Perfectionism is a conceptual holodeck. A perfectionist lives in two worlds—a real one and the ideal one.

Exercise: Leave the Holodeck of Perfectionism

Face it: there is no holographic parallel or second life. Just this one. So, here's another reality check: everything that exists is real, and everything that doesn't exist isn't. If you're looking for a brave new world, visit this one. Pledge allegiance to reality for one day. Live a single day in the perfectly imperfect reality that we all share. Broaden the horizon of your expectations. Write down what you are likely to expect: traffic jams, people being late, bills in the mail, milk that has gone sour, poor cell phone connectivity. Step out of the abstract.

As a perfectionist, you have a case of double vision: you see *what should be* superimposed on *what is*. You are looking at your own thoughts about life, not at life itself. Take this double-vision blur out of your perspective: practice *one view*.

Exercise: One View

Several times a day, look around you and accept whatever you see as being the only way it can be right now. Remind yourself that it is what it is, however imperfect it seems in comparison to your vision of what should be. This will allow you to minimize your frustration with the reality of what is.

In his book *Perfectionism*, Thomas Hurka notes, "real-world achievement lines are hardly straight" (1993, 91). Here's an exercise that might help illuminate this sobering statement.

Exercise: The Circle of Right and Wrong

Find a field or open space (a backyard, a basketball court, or a parking lot). You'll need two markers: two sticks, two bricks, or two empty soda cans. Place one marker anywhere you like, to mark a spot. This spot is going to be your "here." Take another marker and place it thirty or so feet away from your "here." The second marker marks a "there."

Now, let me set up some context. Perfectionism—like all life—is a journey from here to there, from wherever you are to some goal or end-point (some "there"). In this exercise, there will be three scenarios to try.

Path 1. *Position yourself "here" and look at your "there." Your goal is to get from here to there. Turn right 90 degrees, all the way to your right, so that your there is to your left. While still at your here but turned right, look at your there, which is to your left. Important tip: face straight ahead but notice your there with your left eye. See your goal using your peripheral vision. Good. Now start walking forward toward your there, toward your goal, while keeping it in your view. What you will discover is that you are following a curve, as if you are walking in a circle. As you follow this curve, notice that while you are to the right of your goal you are moving—at a curve—to the left. As you walk this right-to-left curve toward your destination, consider the question, "Am I moving right or left? Perhaps both?" Ponder this.*

Path 2. *Same as Path 1, but in reverse. Start at your here point. Turn left. See the goal of there in your right peripheral vision. Start walking toward your goal, pondering whether you are going right or left or both at the same time. Repeat it a few times for additional insights.*

Path 3. *There's more than one way to get from any here to any there. You might disagree and point to a straight line, saying, "If I'm here and I want to get there, then all I have to do is walk in a straight line from here to there." Now that is exactly what perfectionism is all about! True, as far as this exercise goes, you can go from here to there in a straight line because it's an empty field. But life's not like that: there are always obstacles. Try this: walk a few feet from your starting point toward your goal and stop. If this were real life, not just an empty field of possibilities, you would probably* *encounter an obstacle on your way to your goal. You'd have to maneuver around the obstacle. You'd have to now turn left or right and then move in a curvilinear trajectory of both walking away and walking toward your goal, acting both right and wrong at the same time. When we happen upon an obstacle in life, we have to choose between two unknowns. The question of where you should go from here is pointless. There are no shoulds that are custom-made for you, for this point in time, for this interplay of life and your consciousness. Unlike in this empty field, in real life we rarely have the luxury of waiting until a perfect path somehow clears its way for us. In real life, we have to keep on moving: time doesn't wait. Under such conditions, it doesn't matter which way you go because there is no one perfect path. You've heard it before: there is more than one road to Rome. So go ahead: turn right or left. Meditate on this relativity of right and left and right and wrong as you finish this exercise. Walk a few feet, pause to meditate, then choose to turn left or right. Keep your eyes on the goal and walk again. Practice suspending the moral righteousness of your navigation. There is no one ideal path. The map of ideals has nothing to do with the actual topography of life. You can't generalize ideals from one situation to another, from one mind to another. Ideals fail to reflect the unique internal and external obstacles that materialize at a given point in time for a given mind. The realistically optimal path exists only once—right here, right now, and only for you. You cannot know it in advance. You can't learn it from anyone. No one has yet walked that perfect life-line of yours yet. It's up to you to map out your journey.*

self-acceptance manifesto

1.

We confuse perfection with imperfection

But there is no difference

Unless, of course, you compare *what is* with *what isn't*.

2.

If I could be right this very moment better, worse or other than what I am right now

I wouldn't be myself.

But I am, *perfectly imperfect*.

3.

And so are you!

4.

It is always like that, not just during *this* now

But *at any now* that you are alive.

Present *is* perfect.

conclusion: ordinary perfection

By rejecting the perfection of the present, you're also rejecting the perfection of the past. When you reject what is, it's because you think that a given slice of reality could have been better. You believe that what happened didn't have to happen and what didn't happen should have. This kind of thinking is a *false vision of history* in which you believe that there could have been two equally likely versions of events: the one that actually took place and an alternative one, a better one that should have taken place. As a perfectionist you believe that this alternative version of history had the same (if not even better) odds of taking place as the actual version of history. As a result you feel frustrated, befallen by misfortune, and unlucky. But reality doesn't shortchange us. Reality manifests in its entirety without holding back. The universe doesn't save up better versions of itself for a better time. Its timing is...perfect. Each moment of reality, whether it fits with our expectations of what should be happening or not, is the version of reality that had the highest likelihood of occurring at this particular moment; otherwise, it wouldn't have materialized in the first place. Reality is always at its best at any given point in time. And so are you—in a constant flow of *ordinary perfection*. Ordinary perfection is a match between what we think should be and what is. To see it we have to keep recalibrating our expectations (our theories of reality) to match the reality of what is. Or, to express the same idea in reverse (and to once again quote Alexander Pope), *whatever is, is right* (should be). Broaden and update the goals of your perfectionism: in addition to striving for what should be, aim high to notice the ordinary perfection of what is. Strive for acceptance.

CHAPTER 3

perfectly imperfect: from dualities and dichotomies to suchness

Dualism is the real root of our suffering and of all our conflicts.

—Chogyal Namkhai Norbu

When the mind does not discriminate, all things are as they really are. Entering the deep mystery of this suchness releases us from all our attachments.

—Seng-ts'an

S emantics is the study of meaning. In chapter 2 we took a semantic path to redefining perfection by extending the meaning of
the word "perfection" to everything that is. In so doing, we have laid
half the foundation for acceptance of what is. The second half of this
foundation has to do with overcoming the so-called dichotomous
(all-or-nothing, black-and-white) thinking that plagues perfectionistic minds. The goal of this chapter is to learn how to step away from
the language that fuels dichotomous thinking. Thus, we will take a
more scenic path to redefining perfection—a non-semantic path, a
path that takes us beyond language, beyond meaning, beyond comparison, and therefore beyond dichotomies.

language stands in the way of experience

Language is divisive. While, as a vehicle of communication, language
unites the minds of the speakers, it separates the speakers from the
very reality that they are communicating about. You see, every word
is an attempt to describe, distinguish, define, separate, and isolate
a certain aspect of reality. As tools of description, words are selec-
tive: they focus on one aspect of reality and ignore the rest; they
divide and fragment the whole. It's as though the entire language
tries to grasp the whole of reality but, like Edward Scissorhands,
cuts everything it touches, dividing the oneness of reality into infin-
itesimal semantic parts one word at a time. But not all words cut
the same: whereas some are scalpels of precision, others are meant
for a butcher block.

The perfectionistic mind thinks in terms of either/or—dichoto-
mously or dualistically. The word "dichotomy" takes its origin from
the Greek *dicha* (which means "in two") and *temnein* (which means
"to cut") (Online Etymology Dictionary). *Dichotomies* are made of
two mutually exclusive alternatives. Dichotomies are conceptual
scissors that divide one and the same reality in half. Life is *either*
perfect *or* imperfect, a course of action is *either* right *or* wrong,
a person is *either* good *or* bad. Dichotomies are a forced choice
between "this" or "that." As such, dichotomies—by splitting reality

in half—feed desire with pseudo-options. If you are efficient in the morning and inefficient in the afternoon, then you are *both* efficient and inefficient throughout the day. If you ignore the fact that you are efficient in the morning, you'd have to conclude that you are inefficient. That's not a whole picture. However, if you divide the reality of your daily mental performance in half like this, then you are creating a false choice—a choice of being either sharp or dull, efficient or inefficient. This choice doesn't really exist, except in your dualistic, dichotomous mind. Eventually, the dualistic mind falls on its own sword: once you have this perceived choice of being either sharp or dull, you begin to desire one option over another. A desire is a wish for an alternative. Therefore, dichotomies taunt our appetite for perfection, for improvement, for betterment, for the alternative to what is—which leads us to reject the reality of what is and to crave some better reality.

Dichotomies, in dividing reality in half, dangerously oversimplify it, reducing the resolution of our perception to a few basic crude distinctions. George Orwell, in his famous dystopian novel *Nineteen Eighty-Four,* offers a powerful example of the mind-killing effect of dichotomies (1949). In an attempt to prevent *crimethink* (free thought and dissent), the Party introduces *Newspeak,* a language designed to remove the subtleties of meaning by eradicating synonyms and antonyms, leaving speakers with colorless all-or-nothing, black-and-white dichotomies (like "good/ungood," "crimethink/goodthink"). As Newspeak dictionaries shrank with each new edition, so did the minds of the speakers. In some ways, the dichotomy-driven language of perfectionism operates with totalitarian rigidity. If, say, the entire range of grades on an exam were to be reduced to "A/not-A," then an A-minus becomes a not-A. In reducing reality to extremes, dichotomies reduce our reactions to extremes, allowing for no nuance of meaning or understanding.

Because they prohibit shades of meaning, dichotomies come pre-loaded with interpretation. Say your boss asks you to perform a certain task. Regardless of whether your performance will satisfy your boss or not, you know in advance that unless you think your performance is perfect, you won't be satisfied. You've come to equate the meaning of success with "not-failure" or "un-failure." You are either a failure or a not-failure. If that's the meaning you assigned to the notion of success, it's no wonder you never really feel successful. You're only someone who once again didn't fail. So, of course there's never any reason to celebrate or allow yourself anything more than a sigh of relief.

sewing together what's been cut apart

Whereas dichotomous or dualistic thinking cuts and divides reality into subjective notions of perfect and imperfect, of what should and shouldn't be, a non-dual/non-dichotomous (unified) view sews what has been split back together and allows you to perceive reality such as it is, without comparing it to what it is not.

Suchness

In his book *Zen and the Brain*, James Austin introduces the concept of suchness this way: Say we saw "an ordinary pebble... In the first milliseconds of this seeing act, we begin to discriminate the various properties of the object—its size, its color. Almost instantaneously we develop an aesthetic judgment of this object: we either like it or not." Austin asks: "What happened to the stone itself" in this process of evaluation? "The pebble got lost. For its true suchness is none of these extra, human layers." This pebble "existed in its own way, in its *essential namelessness*." "In itself, [it] had no need" to be "tagged by some label." The pebble is neither perfect nor imperfect. The pebble is still part of the universe undivided by the artificial, arbitrary, and fundamentally subjective dichotomies of our minds. It just *is*, "in its suchness" (2001, 549).

From "Or" to "And"

Whereas the word "or" is a dividing sword of dichotomy, the semantic agent of rejection, the word "and" is the semantic glue of acceptance. You are this *and* that. You have both studied hard *and* gotten a C. You both want to accept yourself and are afraid to do it in fear of never meeting your ambitious goals. You are both stuck right now and capable of change in the future. Whereas the word "or" unnecessarily dichotomizes reality into false alternatives, sifting one and the same reality into arbitrarily polarized categories, the word "and" opens you up to acceptance of reality in its entirety.

The Only Truth: "It Is What It Is"

By trying to avoid mistakes and do the "right" thing, you are using a set of personal commandments of what should and should not be. The problem is that by accepting one part of reality and rejecting the other part, you're creating *two realities out of one*: one being the reality that you approve of and the other being the reality that you reject. This dualistic perspective results in two truths: This, here, is perfect. And that, over there, is imperfect.

But this and that are part of one and the same reality. And, indeed, when you and I look at one and the same object of reality (say a hat), and you think it's great looking and I think it's heinous, the only thing that both of us can agree on is that it is what it is. "It is what it is" is the only truth that allows both of us to be right. By proclaiming that it is what it is, we both rise above our subjective aesthetics and acknowledge the objective *suchness* of the object that we were previously trying to judge. We are acknowledging its true nature—that it is the kind of hat that you see as perfect and I see as imperfect. Thus, this hat is both great looking and heinous, depending on whose mind is appraising it. At the same time, this hat (just like James Austin's pebble) is neither good looking nor heinous (when no one is looking) but is a "thing in itself," such as it is.

All truths are relative to one and the same truth, the truth of suchness—the truth that "it" (whatever the "it" may be) is what it is. But to say that something is what it is is to say nothing. Functionally, the phrase is a form of interpretive silence, a form of nonjudgment.

Acceptance Is Nonjudgment and Noncomparison

Perfectionism is the constant judgment of what is against what should be or theoretically could be. Judgment is based on comparison. Unless you compare something to something else, you have no basis for judgment. To conclude that something is substandard, you have to compare it to a standard.

Acceptance, on the other hand, is a noncomparison, and thus nonjudgment. It's interpretive silence, just a witnessing of what is, a kind of experiencing that doesn't bother to ask "How does this compare to the ideal?" Acceptance is an acknowledgment of any given "this" just as it is. After all, when you realize that everything is perfect (in a sense that it is the best it can be at any given moment in time), the comparative question of "is this perfect or imperfect?" doesn't arise as often. The duality of perfection versus imperfection loses meaning. The incessant categorizing and labeling of reality abates, and the real (not imagined) perfection makes its presence known. If everything is perfect, why even call it such? Why waste the energy?

Exercise: Glimpses of Suchness

Sit in silence. Notice the mind noise. Notice the mind noise die down. Notice what's left: notice you. Here you are. In these fleeting spaces in between thoughts, you are still here, simply present, beyond language, beyond labels, wordlessly. Such as you are: neither perfect nor imperfect. Just so.

Exercise: Language Fast

Live a day in suchness: isolate yourself for a day, kill the TV, keep mum, and avoid reading or writing. Live a day in this spacious wordlessness. Notice how all the comparative notions of perfection and excellence phase out. Decide in advance that you will not be journaling about this experience. Otherwise you'll try to "save" it; you'll start encoding it in words, cluttering your mind with descriptions. When there is no audience and nobody to narrate for, the narrator goes away and the experiencer steps in. Be patient. Your mind has been talking for years. It won't stop on a dime. Give it time: maybe a few hours, maybe a whole weekend. A meeting with perfection is worth the wait. In the state of wordless awareness, you'll discover that there is nothing to prove or disprove. Instead of craving existence, you will notice that you already exist. Instead of chasing ideals, you will notice the reality. Speechless, you'll be in awe of nothing more than what just is.

Exercise: Sewing Back Together What You Split

*Grab a ream of paper, a pair of scissors, and some tape. Take a sheet of paper, turn it sideways, and divide it into a top half and bottom half by drawing a line through the middle. Write down a duality. For example: "my car is affordable (which is good), but it is sluggish (which is bad)." Write the good part above the line and the bad part below the line, with the word "but" right across the dividing line. This is the **total** reality of this car. The good part (the cost of the car) is related to the bad part (its performance). After all, if you want "the ultimate driving machine," you'll have to dish out more dough. But you chose not to; thus, you are where you are. That is the total situation. Now, take the scissors and cut this total situation in half, right along the "but" line. What you just did physically is what you tend to do psychologically as a perfectionist: you take a total situation and you cut it in half, dismissing a part of a whole.*

Now, let's put the reality back together—let's sew the halves. Tape the split halves of the paper back together. Write the word "and" over the word "but." What you have now is a position of acceptance: "My car is affordable and somewhat sluggish." Do this once a day to re-integrate what you have perfectionistically split off. "I am doing the best I can right now and I can still try to do better the next time." "My partner is dependable and inflexible." "My work is meaningful and stressful." "I both dig the idea of this exercise and hate the hassle of it." Me too! There are usually 500 sheets of paper to a ream. So get cracking: one precedent of acceptance at a time.

Exercise: Snap Out of Definitional Rigidity

Understand the function of a word: it defines. To define is to finalize and to limit. Find a straight, dry twig of about six to ten inches long. Bend it slightly. Notice the give. Bend it more, until it snaps. What happened? It ran out of flexibility. It's the same with self-definitions. When we define ourselves with words, we become rigid. Find another twig, a fresh one, with enough flexibility to bend into a circle. Bend it. Notice how, when released, it returns to what it was, to its original suchness. Meditate on this. Once released from language, like a fresh twig, we return to our suchness, to such meaning-neutral phrases as "I am what I am," to a language of natural perfection that in saying nothing says nothing false.

Exercise: The Vicious Circle of Dichotomous Labeling

Draw a circle clockwise. Keep going for a few rounds. As you keep going, notice how moving the pen right also means moving the pen left. As you draw from right to left, you are simultaneously drawing from left to right. Keep going around clockwise as you meditate on this. Change the direction, drawing counterclockwise. Meditate on the fact that as you are moving the pen left you are simultaneously moving it right. Think about how the change of direction changed nothing. Appreciate the confusion of this: as you try to establish for yourself whether you are moving right or left, notice how this fundamental dichotomy of left and right fails you. You are not moving either left or right, but moving both left and right. And that, of course, goes against the either/or rule of dichotomy: what's left isn't right. But here it is! Meditate on this for a few minutes to appreciate the inability of any given dichotomy to express the entire complexity of reality. And then ponder the all-too-familiar dichotomy of perfect/imperfect: if you did your practical best but still failed at a given task, are you perfect, imperfect, both, or neither?

Exercise: Define the Indefinable

Words are fundamentally generic: they group aspects of reality into broad categories (such as the category of a "cup") on the basis of similarities (all cups have a certain shape, hold liquid, and so on). But a description through similarities says nothing about the uniqueness of the actual item being described. The word "cup" can never describe a specific cup. Try describing a particular cup in a manner that provides an exclusive description that cannot ever be applied to any other cup. Start by measuring it: you can say that this particular cup is so many inches high, is so many inches in diameter, and holds so many ounces of liquid. But there can be another cup with the same dimensions. You can say that this is a red cup. But 1) some other cup can be called red as well, and 2) the word "red" itself doesn't necessarily capture the particular red of this cup. Recognize that suchness (uniqueness) excludes the possibility of description. Now describe yourself, not your exclusive circumstances (of birth, place, and so on), but your self.

conclusion: similarity isn't sameness

To reiterate, perfectionism is all about comparisons. When you compare yourself to somebody else, you are comparing you to not-you. But uniqueness is beyond comparison. Sure, you and so-and-so might be very similar, but similarity isn't sameness. For you to score like they do (whoever they might be), look like they do, earn like they do, talk like they do, be like they are, you'd have to not be you. But you are you: not worse, not better, just different. To function as a society and to function in a society, we have to play this game of comparisons. This game is useful but fundamentally absurd. After all, how do you compare apples to oranges? Is an apple better than an orange? It depends on subjective taste. Is an apple better than an orange in any objective sense? Of course not—it's just different. When we say "it is what it is," we are also saying that "it" (whatever that "it" might be) is unique—different from anything else. Is so-and-so better than you? That depends on a subjective point of view. Is so-and-so better than you in any objective sense? Of course not. No matter how similar the two of you might be, you aren't the same and the difference between the two of you is what accounts for all the differences between the two of you. Embrace your uniqueness! Whoever or whatever you are, celebrate the uniqueness of your existence. It too is part of the ordinary perfection of all that is.

completely incomplete: a process view of perfection

The world is all that is the case.

—Ludwig Wittgenstein

At any given moment, everything that can exist, exists. Reality is entirely complete. It has no holes. Nothing, absolutely nothing, is amiss. The discrepancies that we see are the differences between the ideal reality that we have dreamed up and the actual reality that has manifested at a given moment. Whether we like what we witness or not, whether it matches our definitions of perfection or not, it is what it is and it's continuously changing. This is the mind-boggling perfection of reality: it is ever renewing, progressing from one state of completion to another, with or without us, with or without our consent or approval. Your being a perfectionist, this stubborn independence of reality rubs you the wrong way. It threatens your sense of control. You don't like this constant change (and resist it); you like status quo (and try to preserve it); and you struggle with a constant succession of unfinished business (and seek closure). Your boss tells you to drop the project you've been working on for months—unfinished—and to start a new one. The car you just spent your Saturday morning cleaning and waxing is already covered with your kids' palm prints. Your MBA night-class professor puts you on the spot with a think-off-the-cuff question that you cannot possibly know how to answer. Life's like a batting cage, and each ball is a curveball. As you try to pause to analyze why you missed the previous one, the new curveball is already on a collision course with your forehead. You feel there just isn't enough time to be perfect all the time at everything. And just being good enough isn't good enough for you. So, you double your efforts. You get up earlier, work longer, take care of yourself less often, and doggedly try to catch up with this incessant flow of reality, feeling that you are falling further and further behind your vision of how your life should be.

This chapter will help you embrace the inevitable, unstoppable stream of life and to flow with it rather than try to swim against it. If reality is a story, it is narrated in its entirety and yet is never finished. It is completely incomplete, and so are you. This too is the ordinary perfection of what is.

the state (static) view of perfection

As a perfectionist, you think of perfection as a state. As you clean your kitchen or your car or your desk, you fantasize about preserving the state of perfection that you have accomplished. If you can only get it right, then it'll remain perfect from then on. You believe that by tinkering with what is, by tweaking the reality, you can engineer a perfect or near-perfect state of reality that will enable lasting happiness and well-being.

But remodeling reality is a frustrating prospect because reality isn't a state. Reality is change, a process, a constant flux. As a perfectionist, you reject this impermanence and yearn for a perfect status quo. This state view of perfection is an emotional setup: even when you achieve that momentarily perfect state, reality doesn't pause to allow you to enjoy it. The moment of accomplishment evaporates as soon as it materializes. But you already know this.

Attachment to Permanence Is Suffering

Buddhists call the impermanence of reality *anitya*. Physicists call it *entropy*. The former witness it, the latter try to control it. Both accept it. But not you. You strive to shape and form reality into what it isn't. You see the natural flow of change as *de-formation*—as a frustrating loss of form rather than as a natural change of form. You'd rather solidify the river of change into an immutable state of perfection and freeze it in time than simply flow with it. In trying to fix the imperfections of reality, you are confusing fluidity with flaws and natural change with decay. You are, in a manner of speaking, a *permanist*—trying to cast an anchor of permanence in a bottomless ocean of change. But trying to attach your well-being to what once was creates *attachment*, a holding-on to what must inevitably change and fade away. Attachment isn't only a loss of contentment, it's also a loss of independence. By making your well-being dependent on the perfect circumstance, you lose the sovereignty of your well-being. Your inner life becomes dependent on the external, on that perfect state of affairs that you absolutely must preserve. You become rigid and tighten up like an anchor chain without enough slack to deal with the ebb and flow of life. No wonder that sometimes, under this tension, you snap.

the process (dynamic) view of perfection

Let's say that you reach that final state of completion, that ultimate state of perfection that cannot be improved upon. Then what? Where do you go from that dead end? Ideal perfection is the end of the line. Nothing follows it, nothing but emptiness. That's why when you feel you've finally reached the pinnacle, immediately after the triumph, there is a feeling of emptiness.

A process view of perfection has no dead ends. It's open ended. You go from one moment of perfection to another and on to another. The process view allows you to see your entire life as an unfolding work in progress, as an ever-changing blossoming of perfection. In a process view of perfection, failure is not an option, in the sense that you are always succeeding since you are always doing your best. After all, one of the meanings of the verb "to succeed" is nothing other than "to follow," not "to do better" but merely "to be next." On a recent tour of Frank Lloyd Wright's Fallingwater, the tour guide said that when Wright was asked, "What is your best work?" he reportedly answered "My next one." Wright, no doubt, understood the logic of flow. In a process view of perfection, you are always realizing your potential. No, not in that perfectionistic sense of trying to be better than you are at any given moment in time. No. You realize your potential by realizing that, at all times, you are realized, fully and completely. You are "realizing" (being aware of) your potential. The process view of perfection sees perfection as a one-way evolutionary process.

Nature is dynamic. Nothing is solid. Everything is in flux. Inside any seemingly immutable object you will find (at a microscopic level) a dazzling beehive of movement. It's the same on a macroscopic plane—just at a slower pace. It is this constant impermanence of things that makes state-like perfection unattainable. Everything flows, streams, and changes—even rock.

Exercise: Even Rock Flows

Find a video of lava flow on YouTube. Watch the molten rock flow. Imagine that point at which solid becomes liquid. Imagine the moment when the temperature hits such an extreme that the rock, once solid, then liquid, evaporates. Imagine rock first sitting, then flowing, and then flying. Then, imagine your rock-solid definition of perfection soften, loosen up, and dissolve. This thought of perfection as ultimate and final accomplishment and completion—it too shall pass. Imagine reality flow in its ever-unfolding completely incomplete suchness. You, rocks, and all.

Exercise: Lava Lamp

*Watch a lava lamp. It offers a potent lesson: whatever is plugged into life is in a constant flow of change. Only when unplugged (dead) does the wax (life) acquire a permanent form. As you watch the wax **trans-form**, notice that there are no states. While it may sometimes seem like one of the blobs has stopped changing, this perception is merely a limitation of the naked eye. If you watched it with slow-speed photography you'd see that its transformation is a nonstop process, just like the opening of a flower, just like life itself. Get in a habit of noticing this constancy of change. Watch a river. Watch traffic. Watch the stream of your thoughts. Notice the perfection of this constant process of renewal that is life.*

A sand *mandala* is Buddhist performance-art of sorts: Monks lay out an intricate design, using fine, multicolored sand. They work from the center and have to be mindful to not disturb their delicate accomplishment. After all, a misstep or a sneeze (like a frivolous gust of circumstance) could destroy the emerging pattern. As the monks work for days, if not weeks, others watch what is emerging. The time to watch the reality is now. After all, there will be no grand opening with wine and cheese: as soon as the accomplishment is finished, the monks will scoop up the sand, carry it to a river, and release it into the flow of change. A sand mandala is a meditation on impermanence, as well as on perfection as completion rather than excellence.

Exercise: Mandalas of Impermanence

Try this for yourself. Make a paper boat and let it float away on a nearby stream. Write a poem on a helium balloon and let it fly away. Stack up a tower out of rolls of toilet paper only to see it fall. Build a sand castle and watch it wash away with the evening tide. Cook an elaborate meal and share it: here it is, and now it's gone. Everything is like that. Acknowledge it, and make your anonymous splash in the river of impermanence without wasting your life calculating the perfect ripple effect of your legacy.

Exercise: An Ode to Process

Get a sheet of paper, a pencil, and an eraser. Write a poem about the inevitable process of change. Put your heart into it. Then slowly, line after line, erase it. Throw away the paper. Not sure what the point is? It's the experience that matters: experience the perfection of the process and the impermanence of the outcome. This poem you wrote is an ode to the perfection of the process of living. Still not sure about the point? The point is that perfection is a line of process, not just the final product. Write another ode to perfection and repeat this process until you feel an understanding that process is the point.

Exercise: Pull Up the Anchor of Your Expectations

By insisting on reality being a certain way, we get stuck. To get unstuck, downgrade your expectations to preferences. Whereas an expectation is an unwarranted entitlement, a demand that reality comply with your vision of how it should be, a preference is just a wish. Instead of expecting traffic to be light, allow a passing wish for traffic to be light and then go with the flow of what is. Instead of waiting for that perfect warm weather to go out for a walk, acknowledge your wish for the preferred weather, then layer up and go out anyway. Instead of waiting for the perfect wind, pull up the anchor of your expectations and sail the wind that exists. Practice expecting nothing and flowing with what is.

conclusion: new perfectionism— perfect the perfection

Let's sum up the key points of part 2. There are two ways to look at yourself and reality: 1) dualistically—as either perfect or imperfect, and 2) nondualistically—as neither perfect nor imperfect. So, there is your choice of psychological software: seeing the world as a discrepancy between what is and should be or seeing the world as it is, in its perfect imperfection, its completely incomplete suchness. The following ten points are a kind of new operating platform to serve as an antidote to the dichotomous/dualistic/all-or-nothing cognitive style that has been the cause of your perfectionistic suffering.

1. A state that is so flawless, so immaculate, so error free, so complete that nothing can be added to it to make it better, is a state beyond improvement. That is theoretical perfection.

2. Practical perfection is a state that is beyond improvement not because it is immaculate, flawless, or error free, but because it has been completed and is now fact.

3. Every moment, by virtue of it being already a fact, is complete. Thus, it is also a state of perfection—a state beyond improvement. This isn't fantasy. It is reality at its practical best.

4. You are part of this reality. You are neither perfect nor imperfect. "Perfect" and "imperfect" are words. You are not words. You are everything you have ever been up to this moment, and no one moment or word can define you in your entirety and complexity. You are what you are, in your suchness.

5. To believe that what happened should not have happened and that what didn't happen should have happened is a violation of causality.

6. It is understandable to want only "this" part of reality and not want "that" part of reality, to want "this" part of yourself and not "that" part of yourself. But while it's possible to want to divide the indivisible, it's not actually possible to do so. Reality is this *and* that, in its such-ness. Any attempt to cut the indivisible whole in half is a departure from reality.

7. Splitting what is into good/bad, perfect/imperfect, proper/improper, success/failure, and so on creates false dichotomies. A false dichotomy produces a perception of alternatives to what is. A belief that the reality does not have to be what it is at any given moment leads to a desire for it to be what it is not. Constant rejection of what is and a desire for what is not is the essence of perfectionistic suffering.

8. To want what doesn't exist and not to want what exists, not to want the reality of the "now" that you have, is a formula for existential suicide. If this reality, as it is in its entirety, is not enough for you, if you feel that you deserve more than this entire universe can summon up at any given moment, then check yourself out in the mirror for a halo around your head.

9. Acceptance of what is isn't passivity. Acceptance of what is means an active engagement with reality. Accept that whatever exists right now is beyond improvement and therefore as perfect as it can be. And, if you think you need to, try to change what is yet to be. As you do so, accept the results of your efforts as the best that you can do. Repeat this cycle of acceptance and change on an as-needed basis.

10. I have a notion of a new perfectionism. The old-paradigm perfectionism was an attempt to perfect the imperfect. The new paradigm: perfecting the perfect. Everything is the best way it can be at a given moment in time—perfect. And yet, it can still be better in the next moment.

The present is already perfect. Relax into that idea; your
work in this moment is done. Now you can look to the
next moment and perfect the future.

Words are the mind's legs. They walk you away from what is.
And yet we need them. So choose their meaning carefully. Your
well-being depends on it. Mind is subjective, and so is your experience of reality. Since subjectivity is but a play on objectivity, you are
free to choose what you mean by perfection. Choose the meaning
you like. For years you've been toying with the idea of attaining the
unattainable. For years you have defined perfection as a theoretical best. Naturally, by these standards, you have always fallen short
of what theoretically could be. You've put into this game far more
than you've gotten out of it. It's time to toy with the idea that perfection is not only attainable but inevitable, with the idea that you
are always doing your best at any given point in time and that is
enough. Enjoy!

overcoming mindlessness, guilt, shame, and motivational apathy

This part is of particular relevance to self-directed (inwardly focused) perfectionists.

CHAPTER 5

the rehabilitation of conscious choice

We all suffer from the same complaint: the conditioned mind.

—David Brazier

Strong desires encourage you, simply because of their strength, to focus, sometimes almost obsessive-compulsively, on one choice or a special choice and to ignore or disparage alternate choices.

—Albert Ellis

Any mind is a hostage to its habits. For perfectionistic minds, this is even more true. The perfectionist's mind is a high-security prison guarded by guilt-tripping "should"s. In a philosophical analysis of the idea of perfectionism, author Thomas Hurka observes: "the perfectionist ideal is a *moral* ideal...it is an ideal people ought to pursue regardless of whether they now want it or would want it in hypothetical circumstances, and apart from any pleasures it may bring" (1993, 17). Restated, this means that we should strive for the sake of striving—not because it feels good, but just because.

Preaching perfectionism for its own sake is akin to idealistic hazing designed to override the fundamentals of human motivation and to override free will. If I tell you to dig a perfect hole in the ground for no reason other than that you can, and you comply without any questions, you are a soldier of the absurd, a zombie. Striving for perfection for no particular reason or gain, just because, is masochistic insanity that can be tolerated only through reflexive compliance. What miraculous force makes this irrational, reflexive compliance possible? Mindlessness.

When mindless, we don't choose for ourselves, we don't lead, we don't self-govern; we follow the shoulds of our programming. Shoulds *are* necessary; to function as a society, we do need guidelines. Perfectionistic shoulds, however, are in a league of their own: either they are irrationally self-referencing ("I should try harder because one should always try harder") or they are extreme expectations ("I should never make a mistake"). In either case, these kinds of perfectionistic shoulds can thrive only on the mindless obedience of a habit. While all of us, up to a point, are creatures of habit, as a perfectionist, you are notoriously rule bound and compulsive. Stuck in your routines, you struggle with change. Unless you learn how to get unstuck, all the changes suggested in this book will be mere curiosities. The goal of this chapter is to help you free yourself from the tyranny of shoulds, to inject some spontaneity into the rigid machinery of mindlessness and help you practice change. The aim is nothing less than to rehabilitate your capacity for making conscious choices. After all, freedom to change begins with a conscious choice.

Before you read on, let me draw your attention to a slightly different patterning of exercises in this chapter. As you will see in a moment, I will be inviting you to engage in seemingly meaningless activities. I assure you that I have no intention of wasting your time. Bear with me and play along. I ask for the benefit of the doubt: there is logic to the layout of this exercise, and it is ultimately to your benefit.

Exercise: Un-Sign Your Name, Part 1

This is a three-part exercise. For now, just sign your name ten times.

the tyranny of shoulds

The word "should," originally spelled *sceolde*, stems from the Old English verb *sculan*, which meant "to owe" (Online Etymological Dictionary). Should-based behavior (what could be considered compulsion) is guided by perceived necessity, by a sense of mandatory obligation. It is behavior out of duty rather than out of desire. It is a mindless reaction driven by the past rather than a mindfully chosen action that reflects the present. It is reflexive automation rather than spontaneous autonomy. It is dependence and determinism rather than freedom and self-determination.

A Should Is a Have-To, Not a Want-To

David Shapiro writes that compulsives, such as perfectionists, replace their "I want to" with the "dutiful 'I should.'" But "I should" (or "I have to") is not an "I want to" (Shapiro, 1981, 81). As a perfectionist, you suffer from a motivational crisis: you've replaced enthusiasm with conscientiousness and zeal with obligation. While productive, you don't enjoy what you do, just the fact of being done with it. You tend to value only the activity that can result in a sense of accomplishment. Only doing something is living, whereas living itself is "wasted unless it 'adds up to something'" (ibid). You don't want the journey; you just want the destination.

Exercise: Un-Sign Your Name, Part 2

Now look at the ten signatures you created in part 1 of this exercise. They are all alike, as they should be, right? A signature is a graphic fingerprint. As such, its value is dependent on its consistency. Now alter your signature twenty times in twenty different ways, making a conscious choice each time.

Conditioned Means Not Free

As a perfectionist, you are self-driven. That's right: there is no one behind you shadowing you with a whip. But—psychologically— there is! In being self-driven, you are driven by a self that you didn't actually program. Don't get me wrong. Of course, it feels like you're free, like you are making decisions all by yourself. Certainly. But let's face it: this self, this list of priorities, this set of standard operating procedures—are they really yours? That's the tragedy of it: your self is serving somebody else's vision of perfection. Unless you critically examine the shoulds that govern your behavior, you are living in accordance with someone else's view of how your life should be lived.

Exercise: Un-Sign Your Name, Part 3

Now sign your name the usual way. Do it twenty times.

Notice the awkwardness of the first several signatures. After having signed your name differently, you became more aware of the process and you lost the mindlessness that was necessary for the signature to be consistent. You went off the autopilot. And now, when you tried to reboot, the autopilot "switch" was sticking a bit, right? But as you continued, the autopilot finally took over and probably the last several signatures look like the original ones.

De-Programming and Re-Programming

What can we glean from the signature exercise? First of all, consistency depends on mindlessness. Thus, mindlessness is not all bad. Second, we can both deprogram and reprogram ourselves.

Third, to deprogram, we have to stop and make conscious, mindful choices. Fourth, mind-fullness (just like stomach fullness) has a residual effect; it lasts (thus the resistance you experienced when you tried to resume the old-style signature). Fifth, a signature represents our identity in much the same way as our self-view (the sum of our thoughts about ourselves) represents us to ourselves. And, just like our signature, our self-view can be deprogrammed and reprogrammed with the help of a conscious choice.

de-conditioning through mindfulness

To decondition your mind and to enable you to be more mindful, I offer you a combination of 1) choice-awareness training (Somov and Somova, 2003), 2) habit-modification training, and 3) pattern-interruption exercises.

Choice-Awareness Training: Rediscovering Freedom

Freedom manifests through the awareness of a choice. But what is a choice? We say we have a choice when we are aware of options to select from. Thus, the notion of choice refers to:

- The awareness of the options available

- The act of selecting one of the options

Becoming aware of the available options restores our sense of freedom, takes us out of autopilot mode, and gives us an opportunity to change our patterns, habits, rituals, and routines.

Theoretical Freedom

We are fundamentally free. And yet, in our everyday life, we do not feel free. We mindlessly repeat the same patterns over and over and, as a result, end up feeling caught up in a vicious circle of sameness—feeling powerless to change. This kind of mindlessness, this sense of being stuck, is true of all of us and particularly true of compulsives and perfectionists.

Operational Freedom

Operational (or practical, actionable) freedom is proportionate to our mindfulness. In other words, we are free to the extent that we are conscious and mindful of our options in each moment. The more options we are aware of at any given moment, the freer we are.

As a perfectionist, when you're stuck in a should, you don't see any options other than the course of action that is expected of you. Your operational freedom is close to zero. Of course, acceptable alternatives exist, but you're not in the habit of looking for them. The exercises at the end of this discussion will help you practice that.

Habit Modification: Powered and Disempowered by Habits

A should becomes a habit, and then the habit reinforces the underlying should. You start out doing something because you think you should. As you keep on with that behavior, it becomes a habit. No longer propelled by the original should, you then justify the habit by thinking that you should continue the behavior because you've behaved that way so far.

The mindlessness of habits saves us time and energy. Habitual behavior is a functional shortcut that spares us the trouble of thinking and the hassle of a conscious choice. As a perfectionist, you are a master habit builder. This skill is part of your efficiency, part of what helps you excel. But, as powerful as habits are, they can also disempower us.

It's exactly this mindlessness and choicelessness that makes habits hard to change. As such, habits disempower our freedom to change. A habitual behavior is experienced as *happening* to the person rather than being *chosen* by the person. That's why, when confronted with something that we did out of habit, we tend to shrug and say, "I don't know why I did it. I just did it." As such, a habit is a foreclosure on choice. Exercises later on will help you spritz some mindfulness onto the rusted gears of your decision making.

Pattern Interruption: Waking Up the Zombie

George Gurdjieff, an early-twentieth-century Greek-Armenian mystic, the pioneer of the so-called Fourth Way, prescribed what amounts to *pattern interruption* activities to wake up human spontaneity from its slumber (Ouspensky, 2001). These include such actions as the use of nondominant hands to perform various routine tasks of daily living. Exercises that follow will offer you some ideas on how to use pattern interruption to reduce your perfectionistic compulsions.

Exercise: The Circle of Choice, Induction

Instructions:

Get three sheets of paper and a pen.

Draw a circle on each sheet, for a total of three circles.

Note: please, do not continue reading any further until you have followed the steps above.

Look at these circles and note your first impressions of them as a group. What stands out for you? First jot down your thoughts, then keep reading.

You are likely to notice the differences between the circles first. That's your dichotomous, dualistic perceptual lens coming into play. As a perfectionist, you are programmed to perceive differences more than similarities. This "difference filter" tends to first bring into focus how this circle is not quite perfect or how it's off center. Now let's notice the similarities: chances are that the placement of the circles on each page is similar. I bet all three circles are somewhat similar in diameter. You probably started drawing each at a similar point on the paper, and all three circles were probably drawn in the same direction. If so, what do you make of these points of similarity? Did you consciously intend for these circles to be similar?

I am about to say something bizarre: you did not draw these circles. These circles, as evidenced by their unintentional similarities, have been drawn too mindlessly, too reflexively, too reactively, too mechanically, too compulsively, too robotically—too unconsciously—for you to take the credit for this action. This was a re-action, a reenactment of some circle-drawing habit in your mind. It wasn't an action because a true action involves conscious deliberation.

Now I invite you to draw another circle, but mindfully, with the awareness of the options available to you. Consciously make the choices that you didn't make the first three times. Choose where on the page to place the circle, the starting point, the direction in which you will draw the circle, the diameter of the circle, and whether to bring the ends of the line together to make a full circle or not. Go ahead.

How was the experience of drawing this last circle different from the experience of drawing the first three circles? What are the different choices that you made? Or did you make the same choices as before but you actually made *them this time? Was this last circle drawn by you, or did it just happen the way it did? Perhaps this time you felt that you were actually present. Congratulations: this time you did draw the circle.*

Exercise: The Circle of Choice, Practice Version

Draw at least one mindful circle every day. Slow down enough to consciously take in all the options available to you at the moment: the hand you'll draw it with, the placement of the drawing on the page, the starting point, the direction, the diameter, whether you will bring the ends of the line together or not, and so on. Use this exercise as an alarm clock for your mind. Time this exercise strategically, before the events in your daily life that are fraught with compulsive mindlessness. For example, if you tend to find yourself on the defensive during business meetings, draw a circle. Right before you go in or when at the actual meeting, doodle a circle mindfully, consciously. Allow this moment to be a metaphorical reminder that this time you will not do what you usually do—you will go a different route. Let's say that you won't defend, you will instead explain (if asked). Instead of anxiously volunteering preemptive justifications, you will calmly wait to be asked; if asked about your course of action, your performance, or your opinion on a given matter, you will explain (rather than defend) or share (without any unnecessary self-deprecatory qualifiers).

Here's another example: say you tend to have a bit of perfectionistic road rage. After you get into your car and before you pull out of your parking spot, draw a mindful circle to wake yourself up to the interpretive options at your disposal. Sure, you can think as before. Maybe everybody really is stupid. Or you can choose to remind yourself that everybody's doing the best they can. If they could be any more attentive, organized, or skilled in their driving, then they would be. In short, as you use this choice-awareness meditation, keep asking yourself: what are the vicious circles I'm stuck in? What are the loops of my mindlessness? And as you identify them, time your choice-awareness circle-drawing meditation at critical times to awaken yourself to an alternative interpretation of what is.

Exercise: Open Your Hand to Open Your Mind

Clench your fist. Now open it. Clench it again and open it again. Clench it one more time; open it one more time. Do you see the pattern? Now, as a daily meditation, clench your hand and open it with conscious awareness of the options available to you. Also, if you find yourself tensing up and clenching your fists, mindfully open your hand both to release the stress and to open your mind to the options you might have not seen.

Exercise: Make a Choice
When It Doesn't Matter

If I offer you a twenty-dollar bill or a hundred-dollar bill and ask you to choose, the choice is more or less predetermined by the pragmatics. As such, it's not really a choice. Now consider what you'd rather have: a red or a blue; one or one point three; a glass or a cup. This offer seems meaningless— and it is. However, meaningless offers represent an opportunity for a pure choice. So when someone asks, "What do you want to do?" and you have no preference, don't opt out of the decision making. Instead of saying, "I don't care; you decide," I recommend that you decide. Make a choice when the actual choice doesn't matter to you. Practice making a choice when it doesn't matter so that you can make a choice when it does.

As a perfectionist, you like for things to go just right without any friction. And yet, friction can be a nice wake-up call. George Gurdjieff encouraged his students to give up "something valuable" but "not forever" in order to create a constant "friction between a 'yes' and a 'no'" (Ouspensky, 2001, 3). So, create friction as a wake-up call to your mind and raise your tolerance for friction.

Exercise: Create Friction

Every day, quit something that you like but can easily live without. Make entirely arbitrary choices; avoid any kind of logical rationalization. Commit to a timeline of no more than a couple of weeks. Here's the key: feel free to break the commitment at any time as long as you do so through a conscious choice. This isn't an exercise in self-mortification, but an opportunity to practice deprogramming and reprogramming yourself. For example, let's say you decide not to use your favorite coffee mug for a couple of weeks. As you reach for it in the morning and experience a moment of friction, you'll have a moment of what Gurdjieff called self-remembering (Tart, 1994). You'll appreciate yourself as the programmer: "That's right. I used to mindlessly reach for this cup, and now I am mindfully resisting this urge. This resistance reminds me of the fact that I'm in charge of my own programming. I am following my own should now."

Enso is Japanese for "circle." In Zen Buddhism, the *enso* is understood to be the moon circle, a symbol of enlightenment and a frequent subject of calligraphy (Austin, 1999). "In the hand of the enlightened person, brushwork transforms into brush*play*" (577). I invite you to practice choice-awareness calligraphy.

Exercise: Choice-Awareness Calligraphy

Try drawing a circle with one easy sweep. Unlike in the circle-drawing exercises, choose not to choose. That too is a choice. Make one easy sweep and accept the outcome of your calligraphy for what it is, regardless of whether your enso is a full moon or a half moon.

Exercise: Break Some Rules

No, this is not a call for a rebellion. As a perfectionist, you are rule bound, stuck in patterns of behaviors. This exercise is an invitation for you to break some nominal rules that are really not all that important in the overall scheme of things.

Upon waking in the morning and still in bed, identify some small rule, convention, habit, or routine of yours that you'll break today. Maybe you'll have a different breakfast or not check your e-mail before you head out the door. And perhaps this little change will allow you to avoid wasting your precious morning time on spell-checking a meaningless e-mail. Or maybe, on the way to work, you'll let somebody cut in front of you without slamming on the horn. This random act of kindness may serve as an opportunity for you to feel less stress, feel less frustration, and feel better about yourself. You get the point: break the rules to update your patterns. Once again, no rebellion—just self-care. The "rules" here refer to your rules, not society's. And since they are your rules, you're free to break them.

Exercise: Endure Unrealistic Shoulds

Ask a friend to exercise some unrealistic expectations of you, one after another. Have this friend sit in front of you and tell you that you should be able to fly, be able to read minds, or be better than you are at any given moment. Have your friend tell you that you should never make a mistake, that you should never be late, and that you should always meet their expectations. Realize that when you fail to live up to somebody's expectations, it's only because their expectations of you are not based on you, on your specific capabilities, on what you are at that given moment in time.

conclusion: get ahead of your shadow

Now that we've reached the end of this chapter, I'd like to offer you a meditation (if you read and visualize) or an actual exercise that you can do if it's sunny outside. Imagine that you're walking down the sidewalk with the sun directly behind you. As you walk, you'll be able to see your shadow directly in front of you. In a manner of speaking, you are following it—it beats you to every step. This is a curious phenomenon. Try it when you have a chance. And as you do this, meditate on the following: this shadow is a metaphor of your programming, a representation of your past. As a perfectionist, you are constantly projecting your vision of what should be onto what is. Your perfectionistic software, like your shadow when the sun's at your back, is leading rather than following you. All of us have the experience of not wanting to say something and then saying it, not wanting to react a certain way but then reacting that way. Our reflexes, our programming, *our past,* gets ahead of our present. As our past becomes our future, we keep repeating the same old patterns, eventually feeling out of control, by-passed by our rituals, witnessing our reactivity represent the worst in us.

Now imagine walking with the sun not behind you but to your side. Now the shadow is shorter: while your programming reflexes still get ahead of you, the actual you reaches the moment of your destination just soon enough to perhaps do some damage control. With the sun to your side and the shadow only slightly ahead of you, perhaps you can apologize soon enough after you snap so that people around you sense that you're almost self-aware enough to coexist with. With the stride of your consciousness almost as long as the short shadow of your past ahead of you, you are stepping on fewer toes and kicking fewer brown bags with bricks inside.

Now imagine walking toward the sun. The sun is right ahead of you. It's so bright you can barely see. There is no shadow ahead of you—there is no programming of the past to lead you forward. So you slow down. You stop. You emerge from sleepwalking. And every step you make from that point on is by conscious choice, illuminated by the light of self-awareness within you, by the luminosity of mindfulness, by the inner clarity of presence. Try this walking meditation in your mind or outdoors some time (when the sun cooperates) to get ahead of the shadow of your programming.

CHAPTER 6

finding perfection in a mistake

I did my best... I did my best!

—Dane Cook

As a self-directed (inwardly oriented) perfectionist, you expect yourself to be perfect. Naturally, when you make a mistake, you are hard on yourself. Given your propensity for all-or-nothing (dichotomous) thinking, a mistake doesn't just taint your record of flawlessness—a single mistake wipes it clean out. After all, there is no such thing as partial success; there is only absolute success or utter failure, right? The usual consolations (that the damage from a mistake is repairable or that the mistake taught you an important lesson) are frankly useless as long as you continue to subscribe to the idea that one should never make a mistake. You are upset by the consequences of the mistake but just as much, if not more, by the belief that what happened didn't have to happen in the first place, that the mistake could've been prevented. The *Present Perfect* view on the matter begins with questioning the assumption that there was a mistake in the first place. After all, if present is perfect, so is the past.

rethinking the meaning of mistakes

Reality doesn't shortchange. Everything is the best it can be at any given point in time. So is everyone. If so, there can be no mistakes, at least not in the conventional sense of the word. Please, note that I have sequenced the exercises below both to illustrate the points I am making and to set up the discussions that follow.

Exercise: Make a Mistake; Fail on Purpose

Fill a paper cup with water and drop it on the floor. Clean up the mess. Grab your house or car keys and step outside of your home. Go to your car and try to open it with your house key. Once unable to, go back home and try to open the house door with a car key. Once unable to, open the door with the right key, get inside, and return to reading. Congratulate yourself on the successful completion of this exercise.

No One Makes Mistakes on Purpose

The phrase "to make a mistake" implies purposive action. But that implication is inaccurate: there are no intentional mistakes. No one consciously sets out to fail. And when we fail on purpose, when we make a mistake by design, we are actually succeeding. Think about the exercise you just did: in trying to fail on purpose, you succeeded. The task was to fail, and you did fail. When you consciously set out to make a mistake, you're trying to successfully carry out a subversive intention. An act of conscious sabotage isn't a mistake (to you), even if it takes the form of a mistake (to others). No one *makes* mistakes. And yet mistakes do take place.

Exercise: Drop the Ball

Now and then we all drop the proverbial ball. Not because we intend to but because there are too many balls to juggle. Understanding the difference between an intentional mistake and an unintentional occurrence is key. With this in mind, practice juggling. Fruits with rinds are best (oranges, limes, lemons) since they won't bust up when dropped. First, drop the object on purpose. That's failure on demand. Now, try to juggle until you drop the "ball" by accident. Alternate between failure-on-demand mode and juggling until failure. See the difference.

even a mistake is evidence of perfection

As a perfectionist, you think of mistakes as evidence of imperfection. But even a mistake is evidence of perfection. After all, with the exception of the mistake that's made on purpose, a mistake is either a mismatch of expectations or an accident. That's all!

A Difference Between What Is and What Should Be

When we think of a mistake, we think of a difference between the real and the ideal. This is the discrepancy between what is and what we expect to be (or what is expected to be). But any expectation is fundamentally generic. Whether the standard is set by you, your boss, your parent, your partner, the legal system, or social norms, it fails to reflect the specifics of any given moment and the specifics of any given mind. Rules and laws set the ideal expectation of conduct that is aimed at everyone but is based on no one in particular. It's true that we shouldn't run a red light, but sometimes we do. Why is that? Certainly not because we want to get a ticket, wreck our car, or run somebody over, but because even the most alert of us now and then experiences a lapse of attention. We're doing our best even when our best falls short of the general expectation.

If you have run a red light at least once in your life, ask yourself if you intended to. Of course you didn't. If you didn't intend to run the red light, then why did you? Oh, you were distracted? The phone rang, you say? But why didn't you wait to answer it? It was about a job lead you couldn't afford to miss? *I* see that you were doing your best, but do you? I'm not saying that it's okay to run through a red light. Nor am I saying that you shouldn't get a ticket. Of course you should. That's how law works: it pinches your wallet and keeps you alert in the future. What I am saying is that just because you didn't fit the general expectation of traffic law, it doesn't mean that you didn't do the best you could at that given moment in time with all the balls you were trying to juggle.

Yes, You Did Do Your Best

A while back I had a highly perfectionistic client who, ashamed of having made a serious mistake at work that threatened his reputation, was contemplating suicide. In reviewing the facts, it became clear that what he referred to as a mistake was an innocent lapse of attention. A precipitating factor was his lack of sleep, which in its turn had to do with his fear of failure. This fear was exacerbated by the birth of his daughter and anxiety about not being at his best at work and losing the job that his young family depended on. By seeing that occurrence as a mistake, he was dismissing the legitimacy of everything else that preceded it. Eventually he was able to see that the "mistake" was a logical inevitability. He was a perfectionist. He had to be, to survive his perfectionistic father. Therefore, it was only to be expected that despite the enormous challenges of being a new parent, he would expect himself to do his work as well as usual. He was eventually able to see that because he was swamped at work and at home, he was doing the only thing he had been programmed to do. He was trying to do everything: be a stellar performer at work and an ideal dad. Overwhelmed and sleep deprived, he suffered an attention lapse and what happened happened. It wasn't a failure, but a success *relative* to the demands of the moment and to the resources that he had at his disposal. I congratulated him and he smiled: he no longer wanted to kill himself. He was finally able to see that he had done his best.

Mistakes Are Accidents

On September 15, 1927, the legendary American dancer Isadora Duncan "met a tragic death" when she "was hurled in an extraordinary manner from an open automobile in which she was riding and instantly killed by the force of her fall to the stone pavement" (The New York Times, 1927). Gertrude Stein, in referring to this occurrence, said "affectations can be dangerous." True: this wouldn't have happened if it had not been for Ms. Duncan's affection for long, flowing scarves and for Benoit Falchetto, whose car she was in. But it's preposterous to imply that Isadora Duncan should not have worn scarves or been in a car with a lover. She wasn't killed by affectations. She was killed by an accident of life. An accident is a collision of variables that cannot be reasonably anticipated. Mistakes are accidents. That's why, if you run through a red light and have a wreck, we first compassionately call it an accident. And only at a later point, for reasons of litigious finger-pointing and compensation, we switch to the blame-game language of wrongdoing.

Exercise: Perfection Treasure Hunt

Identify the three worst mistakes of your life. Find perfection in what appears to be a mistake by unraveling the determinism of what was by applying the following line of thought to each and every one of these three episodes: "If a mistake happened, it had to happen. If it had to happen, it was necessary. If it was necessary, that was the best that could be. If it's the best that could be, then how can it be a mistake?" Practice this line of thought whenever appropriate. It will help you curb your perfectionistic self-loathing and serve as a step toward self-acceptance.

Exercise: Shoulda, Coulda, Woulda, Buddha

Turn rumination into acceptance. Upgrade your perfectionistic "shoulda, coulda, woulda" mantra with the word "buddha." The word buddha means "awakened, enlightened" in Pali. Use this term in its lowercase connotation as a symbol of acceptance and appreciation of the natural perfection of what is. When you find yourself ruminating on some past imperfection, toss a little bit of buddha into your self-talk. Recognize that whatever you did, you did your best, and even if that is not enough for others, it is enough for you. What else could you have done—be better than you were at that moment in time? Wake up to the impossibility of that. Shoulda, coulda, woulda, buddha. End of story.

Exercise: Accept the Learning Curve

Back to the juggling exercise for a moment. I bet when you dropped one of the objects you were juggling you didn't criticize yourself (unless you happen to be a professional juggler). You probably attributed your inability to keep the balls in the air to the complexity of the task. In other words, you accepted the learning curve. Commit to learning a difficult skill (like juggling, or speaking a foreign language) and accept the learning curve ahead. Decide in advance to think of your mistakes as an inevitable part of the learning process.

conclusion: the cup's already broken

You may have picked up your coffee cup from your desk without even looking and brought the cup with surgical precision to your lips a thousand times. But it's only a matter of time before some hidden variable (say, an unforeseen hypoglycemic tremor of your hand) will interfere with your intention to have a sip. As a result, the cup will tip, the coffee will spill onto your crotch, you will yelp and reflexively release your grip, and the cup will drop, smashing on the floor. As the Zen saying goes, the cup is *already* broken. Expect the mistakes, and when they happen, remind yourself (like Dane Cook) that you did your best, even if no one else believes it.

CHAPTER 7

from guilt to regret: rediscovering motivational innocence

Know all and you will pardon all.

—Thomas à Kempis

As a perfectionist, you feel intense dissatisfaction with yourself after a mistake and probably go through such self-conscious emotions as guilt, embarrassment, self-disgust, and even shame. You feel that you let yourself and everyone else down. These painful emotions linger. They may trigger bouts of depression and pave the way for chronic anxiety and worry. Furthermore, guilt, embarrassment, and shame prompt bouts of redemptive striving in order to compensate for your mistakes and imperfections. This is a vicious circle. Here's how it often goes: you make a mistake, you feel ashamed, and you decide to strive harder to make up for your imperfection. You set a more ambitious goal that is even harder to reach, the memory of past mistakes creates performance anxiety, and you make another mistake. You feel even more ashamed and guilt ridden; you withdraw, snap, or maybe "self-medicate" (for example, with alcohol). Eventually you decide to try even harder, and the cycle repeats.

The goal of this chapter is to equip you with faster post-mistake recovery skills. These skills will allow you to be more self-forgiving and to learn from whatever happened without self-loathing, which will pave the way for self-acceptance. A word of caution: I expect that once again you might bristle at some of the ideas in this chapter. I wouldn't be surprised if you did. As a perfectionist, you aren't keen on forgiveness. Keep in mind that I'm not proposing a legal reform or a new code of ethics (after all, the goals of law and psychology aren't necessarily aligned), just a method for self-forgiveness. Any sociological extrapolation of what I'm proposing in this chapter is outside of my writing mandate. My goal in writing this book is to offer you a path of well-being, not to take care of the society that has contributed to your unforgiving self-criticism.

the should–guilt connection

There is a direct semantic and psychological connection between guilt and shoulds. The word "should" is related both to the Old English verb *sceal* ("to owe, to be under obligation") and to the Old English word *scyld*, which meant "guilt" (Online Etymology Dictionary). Thus, guilt is something we feel when we are under an unpaid obligation, when we think we did something we shouldn't have done or didn't do something that we feel we should have done. As such, guilt is an emotional response to a presumably mistaken course of action. But, as we have established, there are no intentional mistakes. Whatever it is that you did or didn't do, it was your best course of action. Why should you feel guilty about your best? Just because somebody expected you to be more than you could be? No one is entitled to that. After all, to be entitled to your being more than you can be is to be entitled to your not being you—to your not being.

the should–shame connection

Shame is perhaps the most toxic should of all: a thought that you shouldn't be you, an embarrassment about one's very existence, that not only did you fail at a specific task, you also failed as a person. That's why we hide when in shame, as if we don't deserve the light of day. Remember that what you consider to be a failure is still a success—a success relative to your abilities. The fact that somebody (or even you at a different time) could have done better is irrelevant. At the given moment in time, you are what you are, you're doing your best, and you're therefore succeeding. So how can your success mean that you are a failure?

guilt vs. regret

Say I offered you an appointment for 4:30 p.m. You seemed uncomfortable with that time (you don't like rush-hour traffic), but you accepted the appointment anyway. On the day in question, you have a wreck on the way to the appointment. Should I feel guilty? Was there anything wrong with my offering you an appointment at that time? Of course not. Should I have withdrawn the offer after you expressed your hesitation? I don't think so. In respect for your self-determination, I deferred to your decision. So, my feeling guilty doesn't make sense. Then what should I feel? Perhaps regret.

Regret is a feeling both similar to and different from guilt. Just like guilt, regret is a wish that something unfortunate hadn't happened. But unlike guilt, regret is void of any sense of personal responsibility for the occurrence. I regret that you had an accident, I wish that it hadn't happened, but I didn't cause it. I didn't force you to take the appointment. I didn't drive your car. I am not responsible for you—you are. It's the same with you: you are not responsible for reality; reality is responsible for itself.

Exercise: Shrug Off Undue Responsibility

Next time you feel guilty, do a guilt check. Rule out malice by asking yourself, "Did I do something that I wasn't supposed to do, or did I not do something that I was supposed to do?" Once you conclude that you didn't do anything wrong (even though something unfortunate did happen as a result of your participation), shrug off the feeling of undue responsibility. Think, "It's a matter of regret, not guilt." Remind yourself that you did the best you could in a given situation. If your best wasn't good enough for a successful outcome, then that's just how it is. The situation is regrettable but nothing more. Say: "I regret that my efforts weren't enough, and I'm sorry that you're upset." (The sorry here conveys compassion, not an apology.)

Not Taking the Guilt-Trip

As a perfectionist, you are guilt prone and thus vulnerable to exploitation. A guilt-trip is when somebody sells you on a particular should or shouldn't, and off you go on a journey of guilt avoidance. Just because somebody else thinks that you should do something, that doesn't mean that you must. You don't have a responsibility to take their shoulds and make them yours. Let's say somebody's trying to shame you and guilt-trip you into helping them. Tell them no. Dispute any residual guilt by reminding yourself that there is nothing morally or ethically wrong with your own pursuit of well-being at the moment. After all, your well-being is no less important than theirs.

Exercise: Go on a Guilt-Trip

Find one of those "save-the-children-from-poverty" commercials online. Most of them are pretty potent guilt-trips. Watch it a few times. If you want to help and you can afford to, then do. Help as much as you want to but not as much as you can. If you experience guilt, reframe the issue as a matter of regret: "I regret that I am not in a position to take financial responsibility for every child in need." If this doesn't cut it for you, go wherever you might stumble upon someone panhandling. When asked for money, recognize that you have no direct obligation to the person in front of you. Help him or her only if you want to but not because you feel you should; you owe that person nothing. If, as a principled perfectionist, you feel that you should help each and every time you can, then consider this: even saints need a break. Remember that self-care isn't an indulgence but a responsibility.

motives, not consequences

You can judge your behavior on the basis of the behavior or on the basis of the motives behind the behavior. As a perfectionist, you are hard on yourself. You tend to focus on what you did and ignore the innocence of your motive. This kind of unforgiving attitude toward yourself undermines your sense of worth and fuels your striving to redeem yourself by being perfect, flawless, and error free next time.

Exercise: Motive-Focused Judgment

Practice the motive-focused judgment approach for one day: Whatever happens in the course of the day, ignore the significance of what happened. Instead, focus on your motive. Of course, you'll have to attend to the problem at some point, but right now focus on the reasons behind your behavior. Judge yourself on the basis of your motives, not according to the outcome of your efforts. Repeat this one every day if you like it.

Rediscovering Your Motivational Innocence

Guilt and/or shame leads to rumination and dwelling on the causes of what happened. At a glance, this seems to be a potentially useful information-processing habit. The problem, however, is that this post-mistake analysis is biased and the conclusion is typically foregone. As a perfectionist, you have already decided that 1) if you "made" the mistake, then of course it was your fault, and 2) the reason you made the mistake is because you're flawed. Let's work on reversing this process in order to rediscover your motivational innocence and to learn to give yourself the benefit of the doubt.

Inter-Causality

Let's say that you and I happen to be on the same subway car. I have flip-flops on. You have stiletto shoes on. The train sways, and you lose your balance, nailing my foot to the floor with your stiletto heel. Now I need reconstructive surgery. I develop a limp, chronic pain, and depression. My wife leaves me. My life is ruined. We bump into each other again and I tell you the story. Should you feel guilty? Of course not. Regretful, but not guilty. It's clear you had no motive to hurt me. But I got hurt. Life's chaotic like that: a butterfly flaps its wings in the Amazon and you have a tornado in Arkansas. Should we blame the butterfly for the devastation of a tornado? Certainly not. But, as a perfectionist, you do. You are a stickler for cause and effect. If you happen to be involved in the causal chain of events, let alone if your behavior is an immediate antecedent of some kind of mishap, you blame yourself. So, if you stepped on my toes, you're to blame for the troubles in my life. After all, if you had been more balanced you would not have injured me and my life would not have been ruined. If you were the perfectionistic, CNN-watching butterfly in the Amazon, then you'd conclude that if you hadn't flapped, that trailer park would be still standing. This is a very formal way of looking at causality. Everything is interrelated, interconnected, and intertwined. Any event is a collision of multiple variables. Each variable is a cause of some effect. But which one is the necessary and sufficient cause/reason behind the mistake you're beating yourself up for? If you had stepped on somebody else's foot instead of mine, would they too have developed chronic pain, gotten depressed, and lost their spouse? It depends on a variety of factors—on their body, on the quality of their marriage, and so on. The final result doesn't all depend on you. Millions of butterflies flap their wings every day. And now and then that one wing flap becomes a part of a long equation of multiple causalities that brings about a certain effect. Your happening to be the last domino in that disastrous cascade doesn't mean that you are to blame. You didn't push the first domino. Life did.

Damage Is No Evidence of Malice

In the example of the stiletto shoes, the dramatic consequence of your loss of balance is indicative neither of the malice of your motive nor of your imperfection. You had no reason to hurt me. Thus, there was no malice. And your loss of balance was not an imperfection. You were as perfectly balanced as you could be at that moment in time. Maybe you're not used to stiletto shoes but wore them for an office party. At the party, you learned about a pending lay-off, got anxious, and self-medicated with one too many cocktails as you commiserated with your colleagues. It's entirely understandable. Your presumed imperfection (whatever it might be) is also a result of the domino effect of multiple causalities. And if you bother to unravel the chain of events behind it, you will find the innocence of your motives.

Using Beginner's Mind to Discover Hidden Variables

Life seems simple, but when you poke around you unravel an amazing interplay of highly nuanced variables that conspire into a most unpredictable interplay. Thus, true analysis of what led up to a particular occurrence requires an open mind. The Zen term for this kind of open perception is *beginner's mind*, a mind that presumes nothing and keeps asking why.

I work with clients to help them cultivate this beginner's mind. One perfectionistic man I saw a while back had a history of depression and was full of shoulds. He was disgusted with himself for having fathered a son with a woman whom he "should not have trusted." Having grown up with a horrendously dysfunctional mother, the last thing he wanted to do was to have his own son grow up in an environment of dysfunction. "I should have been smarter than that," he often said. Having married the woman, he eventually divorced her after her multiple infidelities. He had partial custody of his son and invested a great deal of time in parenting. But his son seemed unhappy. "I did this to him" was my client's verdict, and the sentence he felt he deserved was most extreme. He had already once tried to hang himself, and he felt that his responsibility for his son's problems made his life unlivable.

I helped this client to work with a series of "why" questions to see what had actually happened in this situation. I rolled him as far back in the history of this relationship as I could. In response to his claim that he "made a terrible mistake" by leaving the marriage, I asked him, "Well, why did you leave the marriage?" He answered, "I couldn't take her cheating. I was so depressed that I kept thinking about killing myself. I couldn't do that to my son. I needed to get out of that relationship." So, here he was suddenly normalizing and validating what just a moment ago he had considered to be a terrible mistake. But then he moved on to another should: "I should have never married her in the first place." "Why did you?" I asked. "Well, she was pregnant, and I couldn't walk away from that. I grew up without a dad..." Once again he was unraveling the perfect logic behind what he had thought was another mistake. Having released himself from this thread of responsibility, he fired off another volley of self-accusations. "I shouldn't ever have asked her on a date. I knew she was fooling around, and I shouldn't have slept with her." Once again, I asked: "Why did you ask her on a date? Why did you sleep with her?" He paused. "I didn't think I could do any better, and she seemed like a sure bet. We got pretty drunk. I remember wondering, who was I to judge her? And frankly, I was turned on like hell." Seeing this glimmer of self-acceptance and the possibility of forgiving himself for something as "sinful" as being a young male with a self-esteem problem who wanted to get laid, he immediately jumped to another should. "I've seen what drinking did to my family. I should've been more responsible than that! If I hadn't been drinking that night..." He didn't finish. My turn to respond with another why: "Why did you drink that night?" "I don't know... " He remained silent for a few minutes. It was obvious that he was beginning to see that he had done nothing terribly wrong at the time, nothing horribly unethical, nothing that he wouldn't forgive someone else for. After about a minute he smiled and volunteered, "I feel better." Of course, this was only the beginning of our therapy, but I believe this serial-why process did help yank him out of the ever-tightening noose of perfectionistic self-judgment. Try it for yourself.

Exercise: The Serial-Why Method

Think of a mistake you've made. Now ask yourself a series of why questions about what led up to that error. Track your course of action all the way back to the point at which the mistake you think you made was an entirely natural and humanly understandable course of action given the situational context of that particular moment. When you reach this point of motivational innocence you will experience a sense of self-forgiveness.

Exercise: The Reverse-Empathy Method

Unlike the serial-why method, with its open-ended line of why questions, the reverse-empathy method consists of just two questions. First, think of a mistake that you think you made. Then ask yourself: "Would I forgive someone else for this mistake?" If you answer yes, next ask yourself: "Then why wouldn't I forgive myself for this mistake?"

As a perfectionist, you set the bar higher for yourself than you have for others. You demand more of yourself, and you're harder on yourself. This idea that you can do better is a belief in the potential for perfection. Up to a point, this belief is useful. It allows you to move on: you fail, you beat yourself up, you vow to do better, and off you go. But as you move on, you do so without self-acceptance. You move merely in the hope for redemption. Each time you cut yourself down with your dichotomous conclusion that you are a total failure who, ironically, has the potential to be a total success, you scar and split yourself instead of healing. You too deserve forgiveness.

After all, if you did your best, you did nothing wrong. Try reverse empathy to demonstrate this fact to yourself.

conclusion: self-forgiveness vs. shirking responsibility

There is only one core motive we all share: the pursuit of well-being. We all move away from pain and toward pleasure. It is my firm belief that all conscious existence is lined up along this motivational vector. The rest is just variations on the same theme. How we go about pursuing our well-being is predetermined by the intricate interplay of nature and nurture. Some of us do a better job than others—that is, when we compare people to people. But any such comparison is a comparison of apples to oranges. After all, as I have noted before, similarity isn't sameness and everyone is unique. The difference between how any two people go about pursuing their well-being has to do with the differences between their histories. We are all doing the best we can, no matter how much our best pales in comparison with personal and social ideals. Motivationally innocent and perfectly imperfect, you have nothing to blame yourself for. This isn't some "neurolaw" argument: "my brain plus my past *made* me do it." No. You are not hiding behind your history. You are simply taking your psychological determinism into account in an attempt to accept reality as it is. While this perspective is unlikely to sit well with others (particularly with other perfectionists who may be judging you), it is good enough to set you on the necessary path of self-forgiveness.

CHAPTER 8

from resentment and reluctance to renewed enthusiasm

The deepest craving of human nature is the need to be appreciated.

—William James

While I tend to agree with William James, the "grandfather" of American psychology, on many a point, I ardently disagree on this one. Gratitude is entirely optional. We can do just fine without it—particularly if we can learn to tap into the intrinsic motivation behind what we do. This chapter is about rehabilitating your intrinsic motivation and enthusiasm. You see, as a perfectionist, you are a soldier of duty. You carry out shoulds like military orders, stoically preaching the gospel of "you gotta do what you gotta do" wherever you go. You condemn joy as a frivolous luxury, seeing playfulness as childish and immature. You tend to be all business and rarely smile. You are in a terrible bind: on one hand, you have been conditioned to work hard and to constantly strive; on the other hand, you have been taught to see your striving as a duty, not as something that you actually want to do. As a result, while self-driven, you are to keep your motivations hidden. When asked why you're working so hard, you tend to deny that you want to and insist that you are just doing what needs to be done because somebody (responsible) has to. The result is that you are cut off from your "wants, preferences, and feelings" (Beck, Freeman, and Davis 2004, 324).

In this chapter, I am inviting you to unmask the shoulds to find the hidden wants. I am encouraging you to go on record to acknowledge to yourself and others your motives behind your striving, to make your reasons official, to come out of the motivational closet. By the end of the chapter I think you will be able to conclude that there is no such thing as a "have to"; that there is a "want to" behind every should. I hope that this realization will open you up to acting without a sense of compulsion or obligation, without any undue reluctance and resistance, but with a sense of authentic purpose, meaning, and perhaps even joy. In short, this chapter is about rehabilitating and rediscovering your intrinsic motivation.

a choice is an expression of preference

A choice is an act of conscious selection of one of two or more options. The option you select is the one you prefer. Thus, a choice is an expression of preference. Any choice is. Even if you are choosing between two very bad options. The lesser of two evils, as undesirable as it is in general, is nevertheless a preferred option. Thus, any choice is in the direction of well-being. Any choice, if granted, is a satisfaction of a desire, even if that desire is for nothing more than the lesser of the evils. Whatever the choice may be, if you made it, you freely expressed a preference. What's left is to own your motivation and to live with the consequences of your choice. Not to do so would be unfair to others. If, for example, you're putting long days in at work because, as a perfectionist, you rely on stellar performance to feel good about yourself, it just wouldn't be fair to reproach your family by reminding them of how hard you work. Sure, they might benefit from the extra money you're bringing home. But, let's face it, you aren't doing it for them—you're doing it for you. If you are doing it for yourself, they owe you nothing. Instead of reminding others of what they owe you, mind your own motives.

There's No Gun to Your Head

Each should masks a want. Let's say you're examining the following choice: to read or to clean. You think, "I know I should clean the house, but I don't really want to do that. I'd rather read a book. But if I read the book and don't clean the house, I know I'll feel guilty later when I look at all this mess." As you go back and forth between something you feel you should do and something that you want to do, you are actually choosing between two wants. Your choices are: pleasure plus guilt (if you read instead of cleaning) or no pleasure/no guilt plus possible approval from others for being dutiful (if you clean instead of reading). A choice is an expression of preference; whatever you end up choosing will be the more attractive of the available options (even if it's only the lesser of two evils). As you weigh the pros and cons, the pressure you feel, this tyranny of shoulds, is self-imposed. You know that there is no gun to your head. No one's making you do this. You are your own tyrant here. You're afraid of your own mind, of your own guilt-trip, if you allow yourself a guilty pleasure. But let's face it: whichever way you go, you win. However you slice this up, this choice is in the service of *your* well-being. These shoulds mask *your* desire for approval and to avoid feeling guilty. Whatever you'll do, you'll do it for you (even if somebody else happens to benefit from it). Not an easy truth to swallow, but an existentially essential one.

it's okay to have a motive

Reality runs on cause and effect. We are part of this reality. We run on motive and behavior. We run on reason and behavior. After all, we are reasonable, rational, sentient, sapient beings. If we don't have a reason (a motive) behind what we do, then whatever we are doing is mindless, meaningless, and reflexive. Selflessness seen as unmotivated behavior is a toxic myth. A robot is selfless because it doesn't have a self. A human has a self, and this self makes choices (expresses preferences and moves toward well-being). That's how we operate. That's natural. There's nothing wrong with having a reason behind what you do. As a perfectionist, you struggle to acknowledge your motives in fear that you'll be accused of selfishness. But selfishness doesn't have to be a bad word. Selfishness is simply a pursuit of well-being, an act of self-care. It is our psycho-physiological imperative.

Sure, we aren't always conscious of our reasons and motives, but they are there. We're just not in the habit of acknowledging them. And, of course, sometimes we just do things on autopilot. If I hold the door open for you, I certainly didn't quickly calculate some kind of quid-pro-quo scheme. I'm just being an automaton of politeness. My gesture is reflexive, conditioned: my self wasn't really involved. That's not altruism or selflessness, that's just mindlessness. Having a motive isn't the problem; the problem arises when our motives benefit us at the expense of others' well-being. If, as a perfectionist, you secretly took some work home because you wanted to do a really good job, that action is for you, even if you're not going to get credit for it. How's that? Well, if you made a choice, then you expressed a preference. If you expressed a preference, then there was something preferable about it. But what was desirable in this situation, when you weren't even going to be credited for your extra work? You tell me: you made a choice, you expressed the preference. What moved you to do so? Maybe you thought you'd feel good knowing that you did the best job you could on this given task. Or maybe you were interested in the project itself and welcomed the stimulation of the challenge. But whatever the reason, one thing is clear: you had one. To say that you didn't is to claim that you're an exception to this omnipresent reality of cause and effect.

A reason is a motive. If, for some reason, you like the word reason better than the word motive, then call your motives reasons. What you call it is irrelevant. What's relevant is that you acknowledge—at least to yourself—that whenever you make a choice, you are moving in the direction of your own well-being. You are taking care of yourself. Once again, there's nothing wrong with that! Therefore, you shouldn't feel bad about wanting to feel good. You shouldn't have to sustain yourself on shoulds or hide your motives. After all, a should is just another want. So why the charade? Why not acknowledge your motives? If you want approval for being dutiful, then clean the house. If you want pleasure, read. Why tell yourself that you're cleaning because you feel you should when you know that you're cleaning because you don't want to feel guilty if you don't? It's okay to not want to feel guilty. So, convert a should into a want. After all, it's the same thing anyway. And acknowledging your motives and how your choices advance your well-being, at a minimum, spares you the resentment of acting under obligation and, at a maximum, unleashes the enthusiasm that accompanies a voluntary course of action.

Exercise: Expect No Gratitude

Here's a rule of thumb for you to try. If you volunteered to help, expect no gratitude. Indeed, if others didn't ask you to do what you did for them, they owe you nothing—not even gratitude. If they thank you, that's a bonus. Recognize that whatever you did for them, you did it freely, of your own volition, because it was important for you. Gratitude or not, reciprocation or not, I hope the very fact of doing what matters to you is reward enough. Celebrate the opportunity to act in accordance with your values and priorities. And remember that whatever your reason for helping, it is your reason. Own it!

Exercise: Acknowledge Your Motives

When others thank you, acknowledge that whatever you did, you did it for yourself. There is no shame in self-care. For example, when someone thanks you for having volunteered to assist them, say: "I was happy to help you. I knew that helping you would make me feel good. So, thank you too for giving me an opportunity to do something that I enjoyed. My pleasure!"

Exercise: Reframe a Should as a Want

Practice saying "I want" instead of "I should." For example, imagine that your partner says, "Don't worry about the dishes; just sit down and take a load off." You might likely respond with, "No, I really should do the dishes." For a beneficial change, try acknowledging your want. Say instead, "I'd like to sit down, but I know I probably won't be able to enjoy myself until I clean up. It's okay. I really want to get this out of the way now. That's for me." Admit to yourself and others that however undesirable your options are at a given moment, you are choosing the lesser of the evils. This means that you're choosing the more desirable option—the one you want more. Showing that you are taking care of your desires spares others the inadvertent guilt-trip.

Exercise: Ask for Help and Accept It

As a perfectionist, you might feel that you shouldn't ask for help. As a result, you might have constructed your relationships in a way that feels as though you are the only giver and everyone else is a taker. If you want more givers around you, start taking. Relinquish your monopoly on giving. Share the pleasure of giving by asking for help.

Exercise: Help Anonymously

When you help, it's because you want to help. Getting to do what you want is a reward in itself. You don't need others to thank you for choosing to do what you wanted to do. If you seek credit, you are encouraging others to consider your actions selfless, and that's just not accurate. Whenever you can, remain anonymous in your benefaction and truthful to your motives. In helping, you are helping yourself to feel good. That's enough.

conclusion: learn to want

Motivation is motion (these two words share the same semantic root). Without motivation, nothing moves, nothing lives. Without acknowledging your motivation, you are stuck in apathetic, half-hearted compliance with shoulds. Own your motive and let it propel you from a should to a want—from a life of obligation to a life of desire. Remember that whenever you make a choice, you express a preference. A preference is a desire (even if all you desire is the least objectionable of a handful of lousy options). A desire is a want. Learn to want or you'll end up with a life you don't want. Own your desire or risk being a universally resented, pissed-off, self-righteous martyr. And I feel certain you don't want that.

PART 4

rehabilitation of your self-view

This part is of particular relevance to self-directed perfectionists, as well as to approval-hungry and reflection-hungry perfectionists.

CHAPTER 9

from self-esteem to self-acceptance

It may be difficult... to abandon the belief that there is an instinct toward perfection at work in human beings... I have no faith, however, in the existence of any such internal instinct, and I cannot see how this benevolent illusion is to be preserved.

—Sigmund Freud

In psychological terms, *inoculation* is a form of stress-tolerance training in which you expose yourself to the very situations that cause you distress in order to become immunized or desensitized to them. As you'll recall, one of the motives behind perfectionism is the hunger for approval. As a perfectionist, you have a highly conditional and mostly unfavorable view of yourself, and you strive for approval and validation to feel better about yourself. As an approval-hungry perfectionist, your pursuit of perfection is a foot in the door into somebody else's mind as you try to peddle your talents and abilities in exchange for others' approval. Success, perfect performance, is a make-it-or-break-it issue for you as you base your sense of self-worth on others' thoughts about and reactions to you. Most perfectionists are uncomfortable with acknowledging this. But admitting to your insecurities is an important step toward self-acceptance. The goal of this chapter is to help you become invulnerable to disapproval, criticism, rejection, and invalidation.

self-estimation vs. self-acceptance

However you slice it, self-esteem begins with self-judgment. After all, to estimate is to evaluate, to appraise, to judge. Judgment is when we evaluate something against a standard, against a condition of worth and value. As such, self-estimation is inherently conditional. Through the process of self-estimation we try to see if we meet a certain condition of worth. If we do, we have self-esteem. If we don't, we don't. This dichotomous, dualistic, conditional view of self cuts us apart and fragments our wholeness. And the process of self-evaluation is never over. As we go from one situation to another, our evaluation of ourselves changes. If I play chess with my neighbor, I feel like a king. If I play it online with a grand master, I feel like a pawn. This is the inherent instability of self-esteem: it is dependent on the circumstance and the yardsticks of worth by which we evaluate ourselves. Self-acceptance is different. It is unconditional. Self-acceptance is a once-and-for-all conclusion that you are what you are and that you're doing the best you can at any given point in time. Whereas self-evaluation is based in comparison (between you and others or between what you are and what you think you should be), self-acceptance is based in the reality of who you actually are at any given point in time. Whereas self-esteem is based on arbitrary and subjective yardsticks of worth, self-acceptance requires no yardsticks, measurements, or evaluations and therefore does not allow the possibility of error.

value is an opinion

Minds are fundamentally subjective: we all have opinions of what is but no objective knowledge of what is. After all, to define reality objectively, we would have to be outside of it. But we aren't. To define reality objectively, we would also have to be outside of our subjective minds. But we aren't. Subjectivity isn't objectivity, and an opinion isn't a fact.

To understand the arbitrary nature of any evaluation, we have to understand the concept of value. *Value* (or worth) is perceived utility or usefulness. Anything that has value has some perceived usefulness. Thus, value is an *opinion* of usefulness that is specific to a given mind. Just like beauty, value is in the mind's eye of the beholder. But if value is nothing more than an opinion, if value is fundamentally subjective, then it is also beyond objective proof. As an opinion, value isn't a fact. Since value isn't fact, it cannot prove anything factual or objective. What is valuable to one mind may be trash to another. To one person, a Beanie Baby is a collector's item; to another, it's something to be thrown away. To some, a thought of approval from somebody else is a gold coin; to others, somebody's approval is Monopoly money.

To appraise something as perfect or good or valuable as opposed to imperfect, bad, or worthless is to express a subjective opinion. Nothing more. You and I look at the same picture: you like it; I don't. Who's right, you or I? Both and neither. Your subjective opinion is no more objective than my subjective opinion. Why? Because, by definition, subjectivity isn't objectivity. You say to-may-to; I say to-mah-to. You say po-tay-to, and I say po-tah-to. You say perfect; I say imperfect. Who's right? Values—just like tastes (and pronunciations)—differ. Neither approval nor disapproval proves anything objective. That's the paradox of approval seeking: our very attempt to prove our worth and value means that we feel that our worth and value can be proven. After all, why would we try to prove the value of something if we didn't feel it was valuable in the first place? So here we are: in self-doubt yet convinced enough of our worth and value to try to prove it. And, as perfectionists, we are so convinced of our value that we are willing to go to the ends of human ambition to prove it.

dependence on approval is loss of self

Let's say that after months of unemployment I finally landed a nice job. You are my new boss, and you just bought a new car. You ask me, "What do you think? Like it?" Not wanting to get on your bad side, I say yes. You like my response. You decide to mentor me. I tolerate that. Over time, however, I lose myself. I get conditioned or programmed to look at the world as you do, to define perfection (or value, or meaning, or success, or anything else for that matter) the way you do. I become dependent on the subjectivity of your approval. What started out as adaptive approval-seeking led to an eventual loss of self. In seeking your approval, I got carried away by the currents of your subjectivity.

Lesson learned: to seek approval is to seek dependence; to seek dependence is to lose your sense of self. Sure, up to a point we have to sell out. But to keep yourself from going psychologically bankrupt, keep reminding yourself that all of this when-in-Rome-do-as-Romans-do situational hazing is just another Monopoly game with arbitrary currency. At the end of the day, in the privacy of your own mind, know that only you have the absolute monopoly on how you view yourself.

Self-Consciousness vs. Self-Awareness

To reiterate, self-esteem is self-evaluation (in other words, self-judgment). Judgment makes us uncomfortable. When judged, we feel self-conscious.

Self-acceptance works differently. It doesn't paralyze you; instead, it frees you up. A self-accepting mind is aware of one's self and doesn't get lost in the mirror of social comparisons. Approval seekers, on the other hand, are perpetually self-conscious. They want to see how they look in the mirror of others' minds. They solicit feedback. They cling to praise. Self-accepting minds seek nothing— they go about their business, focused on what's important to them. They're not oblivious, but they are immune to others' disapproval. They know who they are and that others' approval doesn't fundamentally change anything about them. They are self-aware.

Disapproval of Approval and Approval of Disapproval

Not all approval is good news and not all disapproval is bad news. Imagine that you meet somebody and you think that he likes you. You wonder why. Then it dawns on you that he is a taker and that he probably likes you because he sees that he can take advantage of you. You realize that he approves of you for a rather unflattering reason. When you think through the meaning of this approval, it feels more like a criticism than a compliment. Well, what if we turn this scenario around: you meet somebody and you think he doesn't like you. You wonder why. Then it dawns on you: this person is threatened by your intelligence. You realize that his dislike of you is actually an indirect compliment. This disapproval confirms to you something that you do value about yourself. My point? Evaluating yourself solely on the basis of others' approval or disapproval can be misleading. The mere fact of others' approval or disapproval of you is meaningless unless you understand and agree with the reasons behind others' evaluations of you.

Valuable Even If Not Valued

You are valuable even if you aren't valued. Recall that we defined value as perceived utility or usefulness. Even if you are not useful to others, you are still indispensable to yourself. If well-being is the goal, you are the path. You are your own means to an end, your own resource, your own support staff, your own associate and companion. That's your value! That's why you take care of your needs. That's why you take time to rest and feed yourself. Self-care is self-maintenance in the service of the continued pursuit of well-being. You are at your own disposal, at your own service, acting on your own behalf. That's your utility, your vital usefulness to yourself. That's why you are always valuable (to yourself) even if you are not valued by anyone else but yourself. End of debate: your value is a given.

inoculating yourself against others' disapproval

Some of the exercises below are indirect (vicarious) inoculation. They involve you watching other people. You will see them embarrass themselves, feel their shame, think through the situation and the response, invalidate the meaning of the disapproval, and become desensitized. Other exercises involve direct (experiential) inoculation in which you will interact more directly with approval and disapproval. I've tailored the exercises to a wide range of age and assertiveness levels. Try what seems doable. Challenge yourself with the rest later. As you approach direct exposure exercises, allow yourself to feel any reflexive anxiety that comes up. The goal is not to stay calm but to affirm your existence, to set a precedent of not giving a damn. Let inoculation do its magic of desensitization. Run the risk of disapproval instead of running from it. Have fun!

Exercise: Take Your Time Parallel Parking

Parallel parking is fraught with potential for self-consciousness. Even if you signal your intention way ahead of time, there is still the impatience of traffic behind you. Go out to do some parallel parking to practice tolerance of disapproval. Take your time. Risk a honk or two.

Exercise: Rent a Clunker

Rent a clunker. Drive it like it's a Rolls. Roll the windows down. Blast some music. Put a "Just Divorced" sign on the rear bumper. Let others think that you consider yourself all that!

Exercise: Dress Up and Down

Overdress. Underdress. Wear pajamas to Macy's. Wear a tuxedo to the grocery store. Make a fashion statement. Make a fashion mistake. Who cares?

Exercise: Abstain from Me-Too Self-Disclosures

Avoid eager nodding in agreement. Restrain yourself from trying to be liked on the basis of similarity (the "me-too" stories). Let the relationship find you as you are, in your unprecedented uniqueness. Dare to be you.

Exercise: Practice Social Silence

When in company, try silence. Let it thicken. Smile. Say nothing. Work through any embarrassment. So what if you have nothing to say? Big deal!

Exercise: Misspeak

Pick an advanced vocabulary word (such as those on study lists for the GRE) to mispronounce every day. Use it in a wrong context. Allow yourself to be corrected. That won't change you and will help you ferret out fellow perfectionists.

Exercise: Make a Mistake

When dining out, drop a utensil on the floor. Let people rubberneck. They're looking at you—so what? When ordering at a restaurant, change your mind a couple of times. That's not unheard of. And if you can't shrug off your guilt, leave a generous tip.

Exercise: Be a Nuisance

At a streetlight, pause for ten seconds when the light turns green. Let the driver behind you honk. Yes, you are in his way. So? Pop into a convenience store and ask for directions. Then ask to have them repeated. Risk being an inconvenience. The store won't go out of business just because you wasted a moment of their time.

Exercise: Run the Risk of Participation

Show initiative to risk being criticized. Ask a rhetorical question. See the eyebrows rise. Try karaoke. Make a toast at a wedding. Ignore that voice in your head that tells you to keep quiet, and speak up. Take a walk out on a limb.

Exercise: Forget a Thought

When in company, start to voice a thought and pretend to forget it. Hold the floor with an endless plea that it's right on the tip of your tongue. Fake an articulation fiasco.

Exercise: Simulate Disapproval

Arrange to simulate disapproval. Have a not-too-close friend think unfavorable thoughts of you. Sit opposite of him or her and maintain eye contact. Decide in advance that you will not ask what he or she is thinking. Just know that here you are, being judged. Practice being okay with it. Repeat until comfortable. If no one's available, here's a solo version: choose a person (somebody random in a waiting room or a grocery store line) and disapprove of them (think unfavorable thoughts). Watch nothing happen. Envision the reverse.

conclusion: from self-esteem to self-acceptance

Self-acceptance is an acknowledgment of the reality of what you are: a life in progress. Whereas self-esteem is a recurring life-performance evaluation, self-acceptance is evaluation-proof tenure. While self-evaluation is inherently dependent on arbitrary definitions of worth and value, self-acceptance is independent of evaluation and is therefore immune to the ebb and flow of circumstance. And as such, self-acceptance sets you free.

I'm not advocating anarchy. Sure, trying to prove your value to others might help you get a job or a date. True, in this human barter of value, we do have to sell ourselves up to a point. We all have needs and desires to feed. Making a good first impression and being able to meet others' expectations is all part of the game of social survival. The problem is that we take this game of survival a bit too seriously, forgetting to stop playing when there is nothing of value to gain. It is essential that we consciously calibrate how much we worry about what others think to the actual stakes involved.

CHAPTER 10

breaking away from the mirror: dis-identification and re-identification

We usually take ourselves to be the sum of these thoughts, ideas, emotions, and body sensations; but there is nothing solid to them. How can we claim to be our thoughts or opinions or emotions or body when they never stay the same?

—Jack Kornfield

I am what remains, a pure center of awareness, an unmoved witness of all these thoughts, emotions, feelings, and desires.

—Ken Wilber

In trying to satisfy your hunger for approval and reflection, you have been hard at work to follow others' blueprints for success. As a result, you have likely steered far away from who you actually are. Each and every time you have sold out for approval or validation, you have lost a bit of yourself. Each and every time you have checked your reflection in the mirror of others' minds, you have ignored the person standing in front of the mirror. The destination of this chapter is a return to where you actually started out, to your original perfection, to that original you that you've been trying to improve.

The fact is that perfectionism is a common adaptation to parental narcissism. Children of narcissists are molded, not nurtured; shaped, not nourished; customized and perfected to meet their parents' ideals rather than allowed to naturally unfold and blossom according to their own ambitions and preferences. Elan Golomb, the author of the powerful book *Trapped in the Mirror* (1995), sheds light on this common origin of perfectionism: "The child of a narcissist is never seen as she truly is...The child is maimed by endless attempts to improve her" (27). To avoid constant corrections from your parent(s) and parent-figures, you might have tried to beat them to the punch by being perfect and exceeding any possible expectations they might have had of you. Being perfect might have also helped you to feel visible again, to step out from behind the eclipse of your parents' narcissism, back into the limelight.

Even if you didn't grow up with parental narcissism, if you are a perfectionist, the chances are that you grew up in a narcissistic environment that emphasized appearance over substance. After all, many of today's societies are figuratively stuck in the mirror. The net effect of this constant checking to see how you measure up in the social mirror is that you have abbreviated, reduced, and simplified your nuanced but invisible complexity to the all-or-nothing, black-and-white tangibles, to your trophies and your failings. You have, in essence, confused your reflection in the social mirror of expectations for the person who actually stands in front of it. This chapter will help you go beyond surface-thin definitions of yourself in order to reconnect with who you truly are.

in search of a deeper-than-skin-deep self

A consciously chosen self-view begins with the question of "Who/what am I?" There are two ways to answer this. You can describe what you think you are. Or you can establish what you are not. Ken Wilber refers to this process as *dis-identification therapy*. He explains: "as you pursue this dis-identification 'therapy,' you may find that your entire *individual* self..., which heretofore you have fought to defend and protect, begins to go transparent and drop away." As a result, "[y]ou begin to feel that what happens to your personal self—your wishes, hopes, desires, hurts—is not a matter of life-and-death seriousness, because there is within you a deeper and more basic self that is not touched by these peripheral fluctuations, these surface waves of grand commotion" (1998, 38). The goal of dis-identification is to break free from what you are not. As you do so, you will begin to glimpse who and what you are. And when you glimpse that, you will lose interest in polishing your reflection in the mirror of somebody else's mind.

Exercise: Reflect on the Meaning of Reflection

Go to a mirror. See your reflection. Realize that what you're seeing isn't you. You are here, in front of the mirror. What you are looking at isn't you, but your reflection. There it is, on the surface of the mirror. Realize: "I am here, standing in front of a mirror. What I'm seeing is the reflection of me, but not me." Conclude: "I am not a reflection."

Exercise: Mirror Name "Bob"

With an erasable marker, name the mirror "Bob." Write the name right on the mirror. Look at Bob. Look at Bob looking at you.

Realize that there is really no difference between a mirror Bob and a real Bob. And, if mirror Bob were a real Bob, he would be seeing you the way you are seeing your reflection in the mirror. The person called Bob would not be seeing you (as you know you from within), only your reflection distorted by his point of view. Realize that whether you are standing in front of Bob-the-mirror or Bob-the-human, you are not what either Bob "sees."

Now think of someone who has unfavorable thoughts about you or unrealistic expectations of you. Write that person's name on the mirror. Recognize that this other mind doesn't see you the way you see yourself inside, the real you. He or she just sees you the way you reflect in the mirror—distorted, two-dimensional, all surface. Conclude: "I am not a reflection or mental image in the mirror of someone else's mind."

Exercise: Recognize that You Are Not Others' Thoughts

Stand in front of mirror Bob. On the mirror, with an erasable marker, draw a thought bubble that says "I like (insert your own name)." This is what Bob right now thinks about you. What you have here is a visual simulation of approval. Recognize that you are not somebody's thoughts. There's Bob (who represents another person's mind in which you are reflected, or shall we say distorted) and here's you. Now let's change Bob's mind with a new thought bubble: "I don't like (fill in your name)." Ponder the change. Bob's mind has been changed—but you haven't. Regardless of what Bob is thinking, you are still you. Conclude: "I am not what others think."

Exercise: Reflect on the Mirror's Inability to Reflect the Inner

As you stand in front of the mirror, think, "I wonder if the mirror can reflect what I am thinking?" Look at the mirror to see if you can see the reflection of your thought as you are thinking this thought. Recognize: "Nobody can really see and feel exactly what I see and feel." Conclude: "I am not transparent to others."

Exercise: Watch Your Own Mirror

So far you've been looking at your reflections outside of yourself, and I'm hoping that you have established that you are not the reflections in the mirrors of your environments and relationships. But what about when you look inside, into the mirror of your own consciousness? Let us once again do the river-watching exercise. The river-watching exercise allows you to watch your mind as it is reflected in the mirror of your own consciousness. I hope you have been practicing doing this all along, but if not, here's your chance.

But this time, we will use this exercise to make yet another point about what you are not.

Watch your thoughts, and each and every time you recognize that you have a new thought event (mental image, sensation, or feeling), mark down a dot on a piece of paper with a pen or a pencil. Set an alarm clock for five minutes and watch your mind while marking down dots, one after another. Try to remain a dispassionate observer of your thoughts as if you were sitting on the bank of a river watching boats pass by. Just watch the mind flow. See the thoughts come and go down the river while you stay where you are. Adopt this riverbank attitude without getting carried away downriver, without getting caught up in any thought. When the time is up, look at the dots on the paper. Realize that the thoughts came and went, but here you still are. Conclude: "I am not my thoughts or feelings or sensations or memories or images. I am what's in between." This is the condition of am-ness.

am-ness

So, if you are not what you think you are (let alone what others think you are), then what are you? The experience of mindfulness seems to offer a hint. Whenever you pause to watch your mind, it initially seems to flow without pause. Thoughts, sensations, feelings, and images succeed each other in a seemingly seamless procession. After a while, however, you begin to experience moments of pure awareness. At such moments, there are no forms to perceive. You are thoughtless, but mindfully so. Mindfully mindless. You are still aware, but of nothing in particular. Mindful with nothing on your mind. Aware, but not focused on anything. Seeing rather than looking. You just *are*. That's *am-ness*. That's *you*. In this space between the thoughts, in this gap between mind events, you glimpse your consciousness. Or, to be exact, the consciousness glimpses itself. The following exercises will help you glimpse this real you, the you that doesn't change. My goal is for you to recognize the witness you, the observer you, the permanent you. Feel the reality of the uppercase Self, not the lowercase self, the you that is independent of success and failure. This you is naturally perfect—not because you are better than someone else or are accomplished at doing something—but because you are informationally unstained. This is the you that falls asleep at the end of the day after you have let go of the last pestering thought that stands in the way of your rest. This is the you that wakes up in the morning with nothing more than a sense of presence before your mind begins winding up with the stress and anxiety of daily striving. This is the you that you have always been, in between all your moments of glory and defeat. And this is the you that you will continue to remain until you are no longer. You might as well get to know this you. Learning to access this state of am-ness is the process of reengaging with your essential, immutable sense of self. This is *re-identification*. To break away from the mirror of others' thoughts and expectations of you, practice accessing am-ness via mindfulness/river-watching exercises.

Here's another am-ness meditation for you to consider.

Exercise: The Field of Growth

Find (or imagine) a field of grass or a spacious lawn. Sit down somewhere in the middle. Look around. Notice all the blades of grass quivering in the breeze. How many of them do you think there are? Tens of thousands? Maybe millions? Your consciousness is just as vast, just as plentiful. All these blades of grass, all these blossoming flowers, all these bending stems are like all the thoughts you've had, all the feelings you've felt, all the sensations you have experienced. Think about all the scents you've smelled in your life so far, all the things you have seen, all the thoughts you've had. Think about all the sensations you've experienced, all the things you have touched. Think of all the reality that you have experienced that became feelings, sensations, thoughts. Think about all this visual, tactile, gustatory, auditory information that has taken root in your consciousness in the form of impressions, memories, and reflexes. All of this is the contents of you. Memories of all the approvals you have earned and of all the approvals you have lost, ideas you shared and ideas you saved, all the resolved and unresolved issues, and, of course, plans, dreams, intentions, and ambitions yet to complete or pursue. Somewhere in there is a memory of your first kiss, the name of your first dog, the smell of the ocean, a poem you wrote that you never shared with anyone. All of this is part of your growth. But just as a sphere has an infinite number of sides but only one center, all this is a part of you, and no single part of this is you. Somehow, you—with this unmistakable sense of am-ness—are underneath it all. You are the ground, the soil, a plane of am-ness that is the basis of all this experience. What is there to judge about this sense of am-ness if it is the foundation of all judgment? Sit down, watch this field of self-growth, and recognize that you are the field, not just what grows on it or out of it. Sure, you could focus on a beautiful flower and think, "I am this." That would be self-esteem at the expense of the rest of what and who you are. Why focus on one flower and ignore the rest of the field? Sure, this good feeling would blossom, but only until the season changes, until the flower wilts, until somebody tramples upon it. So spend some time in this field. Experience yourself as the entire space, not as the objects in it. And when you are done, leave; go, knowing that all of this overwhelming variety, all these blades of self-growth, all these thoughts, memories, sensations, and feelings aren't you. That's why you can get up and leave all this outside your awareness while still remaining yourself. Take no flowers with you. Carry no image.

conclusion: you are what remains

Knowing what you are not hints at what you are: you are (to borrow a profound thought from Ken Wilber) what remains. When you know what you are, you are no longer easily threatened by inaccurate reflections in the mirror of expectations. The urgency to prove yourself and to earn approval diminishes. Emotional independence grows. And the desire to be perfect becomes, eventually, irrelevant.

PART 5

time, performance, and uncertainty

This part is of particular relevance to control-hungry and approval-hungry perfectionists.

CHAPTER 11

from here to here: developing a healthy relationship with time

Time does not exist as an absolute, but only eternity. Time is quantified eternity, timelessness chopped up into bits and pieces (seconds, hours, days, years) by us. What we call linear time is a reflection of how we perceive change. If we could perceive the changeless, time would cease to exist as we know it...It is up to you, the perceiver, to cut up the timeless any way you like; your awareness creates the time you experience. Someone who experiences time as a scarce commodity...is creating a completely different personal reality from someone who perceives that he has all the time in the world.

—Deepak Chopra

Daily life practice hones the meditator's attention. It keeps bringing its focus back—time after time—on the sharp tip of this present moment. Later, when a major absorption finally occurs, attention also shifts into an ultraclear, one-pointed mode which encompasses the absolute NOW. Where is the past? Where is the future? They have simply fallen off the knife edge to either side.

—James Austin

At this instant, where are the past and future? Nowhere.

—Deepak Chopra

Many of us are in a race against time. As a perfectionist, you are ahead of the pack with a yellow jersey on. In your fixation on meeting goals, you are speeding toward the future, dismissing the present as having only the significance of being a step on the way to a future moment of completion and accomplishment. Ever focused on efficiency and optimization and overburdened with duties and obligations, you are perpetually in a rush, running out of time, too busy to pause and soak in the moment. Punctual yourself, you are unforgiving of others' lack of punctuality. You scoff at breaks as a waste of time, stay late at work (often without getting paid), and bring work home, constantly multitasking in an attempt to pack the present moment with as much productivity as you can possibly squeeze into it. You live for the destination rather than for the journey; for the finish line, not for the scenery. You burn through time like it's going out of style. The past is a painful archive of imperfections, mistakes, and failures. The present is a stressful reminder of all that is yet to be accomplished. But you are in love with the future. After all, only the future holds the chance of redemption, a glimpse of satisfaction. Only the future adequately reflects your ambition and is still flawless in its potential, virgin in its possibilities of success, immaculate in its promise of absolution of all your past inefficiencies. And, most importantly, only the future is still untainted by the imperfections of the here-and-now reality. And that's exactly why you can't wait to get to it.

This chapter will help you slow down, to make peace with time, and it will remind you to partake in the ordinary perfection of the present.

perfectionism is a rejection of now

Perfectionism is fueled by expectations. The verb "to expect" takes its root from the Latin *ex-* ("thoroughly") and *spectare* ("to look"), as in "to look forward to, to anticipate" (Online Etymology Dictionary). Thus, perfectionism is a future orientation, a looking beyond the present. As a perfectionist, you tend to be in the present only long enough to reject it: to confirm that reality once again failed your expectations of perfection and to reset your sights on the future.

Sure, analysis of what happened is important. Yes, planning and anticipation of various contingencies is important. But I will say that any investment of the present time into the past or the future, beyond the point of diminishing returns, is a waste of the present. I am not suggesting a lifelong meditation. No. Just a degree of balance that starts with a commitment to being present *often enough* to feel, when you look back, that you have lived.

lost in the abstraction of time

Time is a curious notion. First of all, it doesn't exist—not in a physical sense. The perception of time is not a sensation, since time is not a physical stimulus. When you look at your watch, you are not perceiving time; you are perceiving movement, the physical movement of the clock hands. Big Ben is just a tower with a complicated device that rotates huge metal hands and makes chiming noises. A sundial is just a stick with a shadow. Clocks are mechanisms, not measurement devices. They have no sensors because there is no physical time to measure. But while time isn't real in a physical sense, it is, nevertheless, a psychological reality.

Exercise: Debunk the Myth

Find an old but working watch. Open it up. See how it works. Recognize that there is no time inside. Or, find an hourglass and turn it over. Watch the sand sift through. Put it on its side in the middle of the sand flow. Recognize that time didn't stop—it's the sand that stopped. Realize that time is a social convention designed to coordinate human activity around a shared reference movement, such as the movement of the sun in the sky. Time how long it takes for you to realize that there is no physical time.

commit to be

You've heard the cliché: the past doesn't exist because it's already over; the future doesn't exist because it has not arrived yet; there is only the present. And yet, as a perfectionist, you tend to disregard the present. You spend your time either in the past, ruminating, or in the future, planning. Now try spending this moment in the present.

Exercise: Refresh the Moment

Wake yourself up. Go into the bathroom and run some cold water. Splash your face and look at your reflection in the mirror. Think: "Here I am. Here it is, another moment of my life ..." Towel off and come back to reading. That's it. Now, don't just read through this exercise. Go ahead: refresh yourself. We'll need a recent fresh moment to refer to shortly as we continue our discussion of time. Go ahead. Plunge into now.

Past Is Memory, Future Is Imagination

Remember the moment of splashing your face with cold water just now? That "now" no longer exists. Remember how vivid it felt to be there? And yet here you are, in a different now, thinking about that now as a "then." What is left of that now? Nothing's left but a memory. As real as that moment was, now it is unreal. And *this* moment too, in a moment, will become unreal. It too will pass into the nothingness of the past. We are always in the now, even if we're spending it thinking about the past or the future. Thus, the past and the future do not exist—they are fictions, nothing but thoughts about what doesn't exist. Consider that any time you spend thinking about something that doesn't exist, that's time spent *not* thinking about what does exist. Any time you are lost in rumination of what no longer is or in the dread of what just might exist, you are lost.

Being Means Being in Time

A sense of being involves a degree of separateness from the rest of the world. After all, the verb "to exist" literally means to stand out. When you are present, your awareness of your own existence happens against the backdrop of time. Recall that time is really just perception of change, of processes, of movement, of information flow. So, to be, we have to experience ourselves as apart from all this flow. Being is a contrast between our subjective permanence and the objective impermanence of everything that is around us, between our (subjective) timelessness and the constant timing (changing) of reality outside of us. Like stillness, being exists in contrast with movement. When we experience ourselves, there is a feeling that while we are fundamentally the same from moment to moment, the world outside of us is changing. We begin to be. We feel reborn. We pop out of the incessant stream of associative and conditioned thinking and mindless behavior. We reconnect with that immutable sense of am-ness. No longer lost in the world, we begin to experience ourselves in a relationship with it. We begin to register the experience. We remember that we are alive. We feel glad that we woke up and marvel at how time has slipped away. Thus, to be, we have to slow down enough to notice ourselves being in time.

Mindlessness Is a Lapse of Time

How often have you looked back at the past week and couldn't remember it? Sure, you can look through your daily planner and even come up with an alibi if you needed to. But don't all these memories seem devoid of that first-person experience of being there? It's as if you know you did this or that, but you don't have the memory of experiencing it. Mindlessness is a time lapse.

Timefulness of Mindfulness

James Austin contrasts ordinary sitting with sitting in mediation (*zazen*). He notes that "ordinary" sitting, in retrospect, "shrinks the estimate of time." "[T]hirty seconds of real time contract so that they seem to last only twenty-six seconds," whereas "during zazen, meditators tend to expand their estimates of time … thirty seconds of real time now seem to last thirty-seven seconds" (1999, 563). Why would that be? It's because meditators, unlike "ordinary" sitters, sit in a state of mindful observation of what is, paying attention, encoding more experience and thus *getting more life out of the same thirty seconds than the rest of us*. The more experience you pack into a period of time, the longer the period of time feels when you look back at it. Mindfulness is, thus, timefulness.

Timelessness of Mindfulness

Mindfulness is also timelessness. After you spend a whole day in mindless frenzy and look back, it feels like time slipped through your fingers. But while you're moving through this frenzied day, you are constantly checking time, racing and waiting, racing and waiting (on the kettle to boil, on the kids to get dressed, on the car in front of you to turn). This is the experience of time in the rat race: while you're in it, time races and drags; and when you look back, you wonder where the time has gone. If you are approaching the day with attention, mindfulness, and presence, you feel timeless as you move through your day. Timelessness isn't when time stops. Timelessness is when you stop paying attention to time. When you're mindfully engaged in reality, you ignore time; you are just doing what you're doing. And when you look back at the day, you see a long, fruitful span of meaning and presence, full of encoded experiences. That's what I call a healthy relationship with time.

Intensity, Information Processing, and Time

There's a good chance you have a pretty vivid memory of where you were on September 11, 2001. Mindfulness, whichever way you come by it (through trauma, a peak experience, or meditation), changes the way you process information. By being fully alive and anchored in the present, we notice every detail. Psychologists call it the "flashbulb effect." When something intense happens, it awakens us and dilates our experience of time, unambiguously anchoring us in the present. We go off autopilot and start paying attention. Whether it's due to a meditative absorption or to something momentous, when "attention has been held *transfixed* for several seconds in this manner, the data become deeply imprinted" (Austin, 1999, 563). Pain is a classic example of how intensity influences time perception: an intense toothache will easily turn five minutes into a perceived eternity. More pain means more intensity (Somov,

2000). More intensity means more information to process in a given moment in time—thus the change in time perception when you are in pain. I am not, of course, suggesting that you hurt yourself in order to leverage psychological time—just that you consider extending the duration of a pleasant experience by dialing up the intensity (see the exercises that follow). Not only will this help you cultivate a healthier relationship with time, it will allow you to infuse some leisure, novelty, and spice into the duty-bound status-quo monotony of your perfection-chasing and perfection-awaiting days.

Exercise: Speed Up to Slow Down

Craig Callender and Ralph Edney, in their book Introducing Time, *write: "[A]ccording to a watch, the trip on a super-fast roller coaster might take only eleven seconds. Eleven seconds might seem like an eternity to the person on the ride, whereas it may seem like almost nothing to someone waiting" (2005, 9). Yes, the day is only twenty-four hours long and yet it has entire eternities hidden in it. Identify personally acceptable forms of intensity: roller-coaster riding, skydiving, paintball, racing, and so on. Watch the time slow down, stop, and disappear. Add intensity to find your eternity. Repeat when you can.*

Exercise: Experiment with Time Perception

Note the time on a piece of paper. Then close your eyes and take ten mindful breaths. Before you re-open your eyes, make a guess as to how long it has been since you started with this breath-focused meditation. Open your eyes and compare your time estimate with the actual amount of time that has elapsed. Try it again, but this time take twenty meditative breaths. Once again compare the time against your estimate. My prediction is that you will overestimate the amount of time you spent breathing. But don't just take my word for it—play with this yourself. Try it several times.

Exercise: Go Timeless

Spend a day without any time reference. Put away all watches. Kill the TV and other forms of media and gadgetry (because they provide time clues) and live one day by the sun. If you find it meaningful, repeat this vacation from time on a regular basis. Invite others to join in.

Exercise: Mindtime

There's lunchtime, dinnertime, and bedtime; we make time for all kinds of time. Make time for mindtime. Pause for a few minutes of contemplation or meditation during the day. See if this slows down the passage of time or helps you to experience timelessness.

Exercise: Tag the Moment

Whenever you stumble upon an auspicious event, take a breath to savor the moment. Pause and say to yourself or to your companion, "I want to remember this!" Look around; soak it in. Take your time. It's your moment in time: experience it. Time-stamp the moment.

Exercise: Avoid Time Terrorism

Avoid "time's running out" urgency ads. As soon as you hear urgent-sounding advertising, turn it off. Urgency makes for impulse consumer decision making. Advertisers count on that. This is below-the-belt "time terrorism." We feel busy enough as it is. Recognize that you've got all the time in the world. After all, in this entire world, right now there is just this now—that's all the time that there is. And all of this now is yours! So kill the TV and turn off the radio. Do not allow your time to be commercialized.

Exercise: Anchor Yourself in the Present

To become more present when doing an otherwise mindless activity, interrupt the usual patterns. For example, try eating with your nondominant hand. Notice how this minor manipulation suddenly anchors you in the present. Incorporate pattern interruption into all kinds of otherwise mindless routines to leverage more mindfulness. Vacuum with a sombrero on. Do bills with a quill pen. Switch up the routine to turn on the awareness. Challenge yourself to do something wild, out of the ordinary, atypical. Create a Kodak moment. Add a page a day to your scrapbook of time.

Exercise: Hyperfocus On Demand

Turn on your focusing superpowers. Let's say it's time to pay the monthly bills. Choose a time when and a place where you won't be interrupted. Put everything else on hold. Get the white-noise headphones on. Clean off the desk completely. Put timekeeping devices out of sight. Get your supplies ready so that you don't have to stop to look for a pen or a postage stamp. Notify your significant others that you are in "radio silence," that you are incommunicado, that you are going dark. Think: "Right now, there is nothing but this. I have made time for this, and right now, nothing else matters. I will not resurface until I am done." Dive in! Lose track of time.

Exercise: Watch the Pot Boil

If you're feeling frenetic, pop out of the time race. Watch the pot boil—literally. Give yourself permission to do absolutely nothing but watch a pot of water come to a boil. How long it takes will depend on the metal of the pot, the amount of water, the intensity of the heat, and the original temperature of the water. My guess? On average this downtime activity will buy you about four or five minutes.

Exercise: Watch a Candle Flame

Watching fire is a primordial pastime. Fire was the first TV: people sat around in a circle and gazed at the dance of the flames. Light a candle and focus on the flame. Burn up a few minutes of time to leverage timelessness.

rumination and worry control to save time

As a perfectionist, you waste an inordinate amount of time thinking about what no longer is. You mull over mistakes for hours, sometimes days. The same goes for future planning. You might spend weeks getting ready for otherwise trivial events. You tend to incessantly dress-rehearse your future course of action in an attempt to anticipate every possible contingency so that you can minimize or, better yet, rule out the possibility of error. Listen: any time you're thinking about something that no longer is or about something that isn't yet, you are thinking about something that doesn't exist. And any time you are thinking about something that doesn't exist, you're not thinking about something that does exist. Put differently, you are missing out on life. Here's how a great Soviet Georgian philosopher, Merab Mamardashvilli, conveyed the existential suicide of rumination and worry: "We often get stuck on that which does not exist. And, in so doing, we cease to exist ourselves" (2000, 353). Rumination- and worry-control skills can help you get unstuck from thoughts about the past and future and allow you to re-enter the here-and-now. As such, limiting rumination and worry is time saving.

Exercise: Accept and Witness

Unfortunately, so-called thought stopping just doesn't work. Trying to avoid thinking about something makes you think even more about it. Instead, accept an unwanted thought as nothing more than a thought, as a passing event. No need to fear it: there's never been a thought that didn't eventually go away. Accept whatever it is that you're thinking about and witness it pass. Practice stepping back from your ruminative thinking or anticipatory worry: focus on the breath, notice the thought, document it with a dot on a piece of paper, and refocus on your breath. Review the river-watching exercise from chapter 1 for details.

Exercise: Ration and Structure

Ration and structure the time you spend thinking about what doesn't exist. Convert free-flowing rumination into structured analysis and convert free-flowing dread into contingency planning.

Set a limit of fifteen minutes. Set a timer and document your thoughts. At the end of the thinking interval, switch to a rigorous activity (like exercise) to shift thinking gears.

Exercise: Open the Fist of the Past

When wanting to let go of painful thoughts of the past, try this. Think of the worst part of what happened in the incident that's bothering you. As you do, clench your fist as tightly as you can. Notice the tension. Think of this as the tension of holding on to the past. Recognize that you have a choice right now: you can stay tense or you can let go. Decide if you want to hold on to the thought or if you're ready to let go of it. When you decide to let go, gradually open your fist to drop the issue. Notice the release of the tension. If it still has a hold on you, repeat this process until it doesn't. If what happened bothers you in more than one way, think of the next worst part. Repeat the sequence.

embrace waiting and cultivate patience

As a perfectionist, you have a bit of a patience problem. It makes sense: the "never-good-enough" judgment, when applied to time, is "never fast enough." Being punctual yourself, you are intolerant of others' tardiness. Proudly efficient, you have no stomach for seemingly unnecessary delays. Whenever having to wait on something or somebody, you find yourself agitated and possibly infuriated. The following exercises will help you cultivate patience and convert the agitated non-doing of waiting into mindful and restful non-doing. The exercises that follow will help you reframe waiting as a gift of time, as an opportunity to be mindfully present in the now, an opportunity that is so rare in your self-imposed rat's race.

Exercise: Recognize the Perfection of Pace

Impatience is the rejection of the pace of a given process because you think it should be unfolding faster than it is. Go ahead and chuckle at this: "There I go, frustrating myself with uninformed expectations about how fast something should be. Obviously, my expectations have not reflected all the variables in this particular equation of life." Our goal in this exercise, in the words of Jon Kabat-Zinn, is to "develop a different perspective, one that sees things as unfolding in their own time" (1994, 52). Choose to release your expectations. Accept any given moment of reality that you find yourself spending in waiting as being the best that it can be. Remind yourself that, after all, if things could move faster, they would. If this checkout clerk could work any faster right now, he or she would. If he or she could be any better trained, then he or she would be better trained. If he or she could be more motivated, then he or she would be. Recognize that what exists right now is all that can exist right now. Recognize the perfection in this delay.

Exercise: Update Your Expectations

In moments of impatience, you might rhetorically proclaim: "why is this taking so long?!" Don't just leave the question hanging in your mind. Answer it. Recognize that there is obviously a discrepancy between your expectation of how long you thought this process would take and how long it's actually taking. Analyze the potential hidden variables. Fine-tune your expectations to increase your predictive accuracy in the future. Update your worldview.

Exercise: Accept that Optimization May Backfire

Sometimes when waiting, you try to optimize. For example, when in slow traffic, you might move into another lane. When you do that, accept the potential perils of your effort. Recognize that in your attempt to save time, you might lose time. If this happens, take responsibility for it. Refocus on the perfection of what is. The lane you're in is moving as fast as it can. This too is perfection. Try to chuckle at the irony of life: the lane you left is now moving faster than the one you're in. Embrace the ambiguity of this adventure that we call life. You never know for sure what's best, and it is this not knowing that allows for an occasional pleasant surprise. Maybe this new lane you're in, the one you have proclaimed to be even slower, is about to open up. Who knows? Accept this waiting as a perfect mystery.

Exercise: Shift from Waiting Mode to Being Mode

When waiting, shift from trying to control what you cannot to controlling your experience of being out of control. Relax into this waiting moment; shift from waiting to being. Turn the waiting room into a meditation hall. Reframe waiting as an opportunity to just be. Think: "Here I am, waiting. This is part of life. This isn't a waste of my life, it's just another moment of my life, and I am not willing to wish it away. I am taking this moment of waiting as a rare opportunity to just do nothing, to just be."

Exercise: Expect Waiting

Waiting is normal. Expect it. As part of daily living, we make predictions about how long such and such will take. But we are not fortune-tellers.

Naturally, we can't know for sure. Sometimes our predictions are on the money; sometimes they're not. Predictive inaccuracy is inevitable. So expect to do some waiting every day. Catalog likely waiting situations and accept them as normal when they occur. Have your "waiting kit" with you (a book, a magazine, an MP3 player). Practice restful non-doing.

cultivate process awareness

I encourage you to cultivate *process awareness*. Process awareness is an awareness of the ever-unfolding life all around us. By cultivating process awareness you get better at recognizing life in progress, seeing the movement of change, and understanding the present as continuous and evolving. The exercises that follow will help you cultivate this awareness.

Exercise: I Like this Part

Deconstruct some of your leisure routines, chores, work activities, and even relational dynamics to identify the parts of these processes that you like. For example, let's look at going out with a friend. Recognize the parts of going out that you like (because, let's face it, most experiences are mixed and not all parts are fun). Perhaps your favorite part is that brainstorming moment of deciding where to go or what to do. When the part that you like happens, allow yourself a thought: "I like this part!" Savor that part of the process while it lasts. Make sure the best part doesn't go unnoticed.

Exercise: This Is Part of the Process

Identify the parts of various processes that you don't like, and get into a habit of recognizing that each of these moments is just part of the process. When you run into one of these moments and begin to feel resistance to it, think to yourself: "It's just part of the process." As a result, the whole process will not be eclipsed by the part that you didn't like. Also, recognize that the part that you don't like is most likely a required element of the whole. Recognize the necessity of that part. And when you find yourself in that moment that you don't like, think: "This is an important part of the overall process." Thinking this way can help you better flow with the river of time.

mindful being is mindful doing and mindful non-doing

As a perfectionist, you expect yourself to be constantly striving. You're a busy bee, terrified of downtime; it spooks you with its existential emptiness. When we're not busily occupied we risk the rising of the boogeyman question: "What's it all about?"

So you run from these big questions, frantically escaping into productivity. Goal orientation and constant striving offer you the reassurance of short-term purpose and distract you from unanswered questions about your existence. As scary as it is to stop this lifelong marathon toward perfection, I encourage you to take a break now and then. Without an occasional respite, how will you learn the most basic human skill of just being? Without the practice of mindful presence, how will you ever balance being and doing? Now, I'm not suggesting that you stop everything, quit your job, and mindlessly do nothing. No. What I am suggesting is that you occasionally allow yourself some mindful non-doing. Consider it existential hygiene.

The False Conflict Between Doing and Non-Doing

As a perfectionist, you probably distinguish doing and being through notions of utility (or usefulness). You see doing as producing an outcome, accomplishing something. And you see simply being as a frivolity. When we're not doing something, we're accomplishing nothing, idling, and generally wasting time. When seen in these terms, doing certainly seems like a better use of time than being. The problem is that a lot of our goal-oriented behavior is so mindlessly reactive and reflexive that it might not have much utility. We're often busy just to be busy, engaging mindlessly without having first consciously considered whether a given act is actually in line with our life goals. As a result, we end up wasting time. So, as you see, not all doing is preferable to non-doing. Mindlessly initiated doing takes us away from ourselves, whereas mindful non-doing allows us to stay where we are and to get a better sense of where to go from here.

Exercise: Calculate Time Drain

Take some time to calculate the ways in which doing costs you time without necessarily accomplishing much in return. For example, consider the case of washing your car or compulsively checking your e-mail. Ponder the futility of this. Your conclusions might spare you some time in the future.

Exercise: Legitimize Downtime

Downtime is essential. Take a few minutes to recall the times when you benefited from non-doing. Maybe you were relaxing in the backyard or on vacation and you were hit by a stroke of genius. Perhaps a solution to a problem dawned on you, or you had an out-of-the-blue flash of insight. Recall these "A-ha!" moments and legitimize downtime as being part of your productivity and creativity.

conclusion: from here to here

Where do you go from here? Hopefully, always back to here (with "here" being a time coordinate, not a space coordinate). In encouraging these moments of presence, I'm not suggesting that you change your life priorities. Live your life as you've lived it thus far— just a tad more mindfully. Try to break up the mindless monotony of future-oriented days with moments of presence. Recognize that the perception of time is an experience, a state of your consciousness, not a number on a clock. Thus, there is no need to fear or to worship time. Own it. Take responsibility for your time perception and manipulate it when necessary.

CHAPTER 12

from outcome to process: in search of perfect performance

The archer ceases to be conscious of himself as the one who is engaged in hitting the bull's-eye which confronts him.

—Eugen Herrigel

As a perfectionist, you dream of perfect outcomes. If you achieve these goals, you celebrate with nothing more than a sigh of relief. As productive as you might have been in your work life, chances are you haven't enjoyed the process of performance or its outcomes. You've likely dreaded many a project, anxiously pored over plans, agonized over details, and overprepared when everybody else was probably confident you'd do just fine. Regardless of how stellar your track record may be, your anxiety-ridden outcome-focused approach has probably sometimes harmed and undermined your performance.

Peak performance, by definition, is *optimal* performance, when "one becomes totally absorbed in what one is doing, to the exclusion of all other thoughts and emotions" (Jackson & Czikszentmihalyi, 1999, 5). Sounds like mindfulness, doesn't it? This chapter isn't about "optimal" or "peak" performance per se, but about perfect performance (using the expanded definition of perfection I offered in chapter 2). The difference between peak performance and *perfect performance* (as I see it) will crystallize as you work your way through this chapter. But for now, let me highlight an important implication from Czikszentmihalyi and Jackson's description of peak performance: to leverage performance, you have to focus on what you are doing, not on the outcome of your action. Process focus, it seems, assures optimal outcomes.

outcome preoccupation

We're going to further explore the achievement of perfection. We'll start with a rather involved exercise that is crucial to your understanding. To better appreciate the point, don't just read—participate. Get a pen and several sheets of paper. If you're using sticky notes, please first separate them from each other. If you're using a notebook or pad of paper, tear out several pages before you draw on them. This is a five-part exercise, and it works only if you do it in one sitting.

Exercise: Draw a Perfect Circle, Part 1

Take the first piece of paper and draw a geometrically perfect circle. Now I want you to rate your drawing. If zero is poor drawing and ten is excellent drawing, how does your circle score? Rate the drawing and write the rating outside the circle. Put this first sheet aside.

Exercise: Draw a Perfect Circle, Part 2

Grab the second sheet of paper. This time, put some effort into drawing your circle. See if you can do better than last time. Go ahead—draw a better circle than the first one. Assess the outcome of this drawing effort using the same scale as before. Write down the numerical rating outside the circle. Put this second sheet aside.

Exercise: Draw a Perfect Circle, Part 3

Now use the third sheet of paper. I'd like you to draw one more circle, but this time, really push yourself! This circle is the last one you're going to draw today, so it has to be the best one yet. Make-it-or-break-it time. Understanding the point that I'm trying to make depends on you doing the all-time best you can. If you need to steady your hand, do. Ready? Set. Go! Draw the best circle yet! Now rate your drawing on the zero-to-ten scale and write the rating down.

Exercise: Outcome Analysis

Did the third circle come out better than the second? Worse? What do you make of your results? If your third drawing turned out worse than either the first drawing or the second drawing, ponder why. Did your second drawing turn out worse than your first? If so, think about why. Review your experience and write down your thoughts.

Exercise: Reassessment

So far we've been interested in appraising the outcome of your drawing efforts. Let's reassess what you did in terms of the effort you put into your drawings. Use a scale in which zero means "no effort" and ten means "maximum effort." Before you reassess, review the three experiences in your memory. Did it take you longer the third time to draw a circle than it did the second time? Did the second circle take you longer than the first? More time means more effort. Did you reposition the paper the third time? Did you steady your hand? Did you pause in the middle of the drawings? Recall the progression of effort from one drawing to another and assess each effort accordingly. Write down the effort ratings inside each circle. Look at the outcome and effort ratings for each round of drawings. Any trends? Summarize your thoughts.

Does Effort Correlate to Outcome?

In offering this exercise, I had two points to make. One was to illustrate the dynamics of outcome preoccupation. By offering an outcome-focused scale of appraisal with which to judge your circles, I attempted to trigger a perfectionistic mind-set in which outcome is the only aspect of performance that matters. The problem with outcome preoccupation is that it can trigger performance anxiety, which, in its turn, distracts from the effort. My guess is that the third drawing, outcome-wise, is no better than the first two drawings. In fact, there's a good chance that the first drawing came out the best (although not necessarily). If it did, it's because you probably cared less about the outcome. If you recall, the second set of instructions introduced the pressure-cooker language of doing better. The instructions dialed up the pressure to an almost comical degree in the third round when I suggested that it should be a "make-or-break-it" attempt.

The second point of the exercise was to introduce a different scale of appraisal. Initially you were assessing the drawings in terms of the outcome of your effort. At the end, you reassessed the drawings in terms of the effort you put into each. Chances are that while the outcome ratings declined or stayed stagnant, the effort ratings increased. The first drawing was probably rather effortless. You probably worked a little harder the second time around. And I'll bet you exerted the most effort during the last round.

The different scales tell you two rather different stories. The outcome ratings in this exercise tell a story of either fluctuating success or stagnation of outcome. The effort ratings tell a story of a linear success. If your outcome ratings also tell the story of linear progress (that is, the outcome of the third drawing is better than the second, and the outcome of the second drawing is better than the first), I predict that the effort curve is steeper than the outcome curve. Now imagine that drawing a circle was an essential work task. Which scale of appraisal—effort based or outcome based— would have allowed you to have a better night after work? Which would have spared you a sense of dissatisfaction with yourself? If you based your judgment of yourself on how things turned out rather than on how hard you tried, then a poor outcome would naturally cause you to feel bad about yourself. But if you used the effort scale, then you'd probably feel okay. If you appraised your effort, you'd know that you had tried hard even if the outcome didn't prove to be particularly great.

Outcome Preoccupation Gets In the Way

Outcome preoccupation is a lousy performance-enhancement strategy. Outcome preoccupation is a leak of concentration and focus. It kicks you out of the groove of performance. It paralyzes you with anxiety-provoking thoughts, diverting your attention from the here-and-now of the task at hand. Psychologists Robert Yerkes and John Dodson (1908) observed the following relationship between physiological or mental arousal and performance. Performance increases up to a point as the arousal increases. But when arousal gets too high, performance declines. In other words, some arousal is good; it serves as a catalyst for performance. But too much arousal backfires.

For you as a perfectionist, failure is not an option. You are preoccupied with a perfect outcome. After all, it's not just successful completion of the task that matters to you: you tend to think that your reputation and, more importantly, your sense of self-worth are riding on a perfect outcome. Anxiety is a natural by-product of this kind of thinking: the more you worry about the outcome, the more anxious you get. The more anxious you get, the less focused you are, and the worse you do.

rethinking effort

The word "effort" comes with the connotation of striving, of trying to be stronger than you are at any given point in time. But that's an unfortunate misunderstanding. According to The Online Etymological Dictionary, effort literally means "a show of strength" (from the Latin verb *exfortiare*). Showing strength means showing what you are, not trying to be more than you are. But what are you? You are your present. After all, you aren't what you were, nor are you what you might be at some point in the future. You are what you are at any given point in time. You are what you are now—nothing more and nothing less than your present self. So show off your present. Focus on what you are now, not on what you want to be. To exert maximum effort, first accept what you are now, then use all you've got, however much of it you have. Effort is self-acceptance, not self-transcendence.

You Are Always at Your Best-Effort Level

You might think: "But what if my effort isn't good enough?" No worries. You are always at your best, effort-wise. This classic perfectionistic concern about not trying hard enough stems from the misconception of perfection. If you'll recall, we have redefined perfection as a state that is beyond improvement. Every moment is a moment of practical (not theoretical) perfection because, by definition, it already *is*. Each moment is completed and therefore complete; it cannot be any better than it is. There is nothing to add to make it better. It is as good as it can be right now, and, as such, it is perfect. There is no scale of zero-to-ten where zero stands for "imperfect reality" and ten stands for "perfect reality." Reality at any given moment is the one and only outcome (and therefore the *best possible*) outcome of what could have been. And you are part of this perfect reality. Your effort is part of your perfection. Therefore, you are always at your best-effort level. Not at some *theoretical* best level of effort, but at your *practical* best level of effort. Comparing your effort to someone else's effort is like comparing apples to oranges. You are you, not someone else. You've got what you've got, effort-wise, at any given point in time. If you could be stronger at any given point in time, if you could be more than you are at any given point in time, then you would be.

You Couldn't Have Tried Harder

Let's say you're ruminating about your work performance, wondering if you could have tried harder than you did. I'd offer you the serial-why method to help you find perfection in your supposedly less-than-optimal outcome.

I'd ask: "If you feel you could have tried harder, why didn't you?"

You: Because I was tired and I didn't have more focus and concentration to offer to the task than I did.

Me: Okay. So you did offer the most effort you had?

You: But it wasn't enough to do well!

Me: But just because the amount of effort you offered didn't produce the outcome you had in mind doesn't mean that you didn't try your hardest at that moment, given the limited psychological resources you had at your disposal at that moment.

You: True, but I should've known better. I shouldn't have stayed up the night before; then I would have been more rested and I could have tried harder...

Me: Yes, if you had been more rested, perhaps you would have done better. The fact that you weren't rested doesn't change the fact that you gave your best effort given the psychological resources you had at the moment.

You: True... I guess I shouldn't have been so concerned about the outcome. I should have just focused on what I was doing, and I would have done better.

Me: Okay—why didn't you focus more on what you were doing instead of thinking about the outcome?

You: Because I was worried about failing... I am a perfectionist, you know!

Me: Yes, I know. It seems that as little as you tried, you couldn't have tried any harder—which means that you tried your best. And it seems that the combination of insufficient rest and your perfectionistic outcome preoccupation handicapped your performance. But, in spite of all these limitations, you offered all you had. So what are you beating yourself up for?

You: I shouldn't have been so perfectionistic.

Me: Well, now you're being perfectionistic about not being perfectionistic.

You: Yep, doing my best...

Me: Outcome-wise? Effort-wise?

You: Both.

Me: Now we're on the same page!

Indeed, what if you equate your sense of worth not with the outcome, but with your effort? Wouldn't you then be more focused, more concentrated on the task at hand, rather than preoccupied with saving your sense of worth by assuring a perfect outcome? Free from outcome preoccupation, don't you think you'd stand a better chance of manifesting yourself in all your present strength?

rethinking the outcome

Outcome-focused scales of appraisal are inevitable. There will be grades, ranks, performance evaluations, protocols to adhere to, rules to abide by, and pass/fail criteria. The world will continue to assess you on outcome. That's the way of the world. But in your own relationship with yourself, you don't have to use the outcome yardstick. If you want a gauge to measure your worth with, use the amount of effort you used. But better yet, skip the evaluation altogether and accept—wholesale—that you are always operating at the level of the best effort you are capable of at any given point in time. If you are always at your best-effort level, you are always at your best-outcome level. Whether your outcome is good enough for somebody else or not is a different issue. What matters is that your best (effort and outcome) is enough for you. And why wouldn't it be? You can only do what you can do—and that's enough!

No Moment Is Bigger than the Rest of Your Life

Any given outcome is an event in time, a moment in your life. No one moment in your life is bigger than the rest of your life. Sure, there are pivotal moments, make-it-or-break-it times, moments of unique opportunity. But none of this is you. These moments are part of the flow of your life. Seeing the impermanence of these moments, that any given moment of performance is already a moment of the past by the time you've consciously registered it, allows you to rejoin the flow of what is. It's the flowing that matters, not the outcome of this flow; living, not life's accomplishments; the optimal experience, not the optimal outcome.

perfect performance vs. peak performance

Peak performance isn't perfect performance. *Peak performance*, as defined by authors Susan Jackson and Mihaly Czikszentmihalyi, is "one's highest level of performance" (1999, 11). Peak performance is one's all-time highest level of performance. Perfect performance is the highest level of performance at a given point in time. But we established that you are always at your best-effort level and therefore producing your best possible outcome. Doesn't that mean that all performance is perfect? Yes, effort-wise and outcome-wise, all your performance is perfect when you compare you to you at any given point in time (even if your performance is not up to snuff from somebody else's perspective). So, what is perfect performance? Does the phrase even have any meaning? Yes, it does when we look at the experience of performance rather than at its outcome.

Perfect performance, as I see it, is performance that feels good. It's perfect experientially, not in terms of productivity. Experientially perfect performance is evaluation-free performance. It is un-self-conscious and self-accepting, process focused rather than outcome focused, the kind of performance you find when you practice, not when you compete. James Austin's description of enlightened Zen action parallels experientially perfect performance: it is action "without initial hesitation, quick in execution, simple but efficient, highly creative, improvisational, yet capable of resolving both the immediate situation and of addressing the big picture as well, expressed from a foundation of poise, liberated from word-thoughts and personal concerns" (1999, 668).

aiming your consciousness at this moment

In her classic book *Mindfulness*, Ellen J. Langer notes that "preoccupation with outcome can make us mindless" (1989, 75). Indeed, outcome orientation is necessarily an orientation toward the future. Therefore, focusing on outcome takes us out of the present moment, out of the very moment in which we have to act. As such, outcome orientation disorients as it disengages us from what is. Instead of aiming an arrow of consciousness at the task at hand, we aim it at ourselves: we target our ego, threatening to wound it with the possibility of failure. This potential threat makes us tense up. We become paralyzed in inaction. Or we prematurely release the tension just to be done, just to get past the stress of the moment.

In *Zen in the Art of Archery*, German professor of philosophy Eugen Herrigel teaches about the importance of practicing aim-and-release skills without a target (1953). James Austin provides the physiological backdrop for this key archery-training method: "one's muscles must learn how to *release*, not only contract" and notes that "it takes years of Zen archery to develop the subtle skills of *let go* smoothly, passively," while "in the interim, erratic arrows betray the student's old self-referent behavior patterns" (1999, 670). To this end, throw away the target and begin to practice *aiming* your consciousness, not at a target, but at this moment right now. Experientially perfect performance is mindful performance, not self-conscious performance.

There Is No "I" in the Outcome

Herrigel's thought that "the archer ceases to be conscious of himself as the one who is engaged in hitting the bull's-eye which confronts him" (1953, 6) can be understood to mean that it is not you that is involved in the outcome, but the arrow. The arrow is an extension of your arm. The arm is an extension of your body. The body is an extension of your mind. Your mind is an extension of the arrow of your consciousness. When you release the bowstring of your performance and when the arrow hits or misses the target, you are still standing where you were standing; you are still you, regardless of the outcome. You were there before any given outcome, and you will be there after a given outcome. But this outcome came out of you. It wouldn't have happened without you. Remember: you are not the outcome of the outcome; it's the outcome that is the outcome of you.

Target the Practice, Not the Target

The following exercises are designed to help you throw away the obsession with outcome stats and target the practice itself.

Exercise: Keep No Score

Outcome preoccupation is scorekeeping. It kills the joy of the process. For example, consider giving up the pedantic journaling of reps and sets in the middle of your workouts. It's a waste of time that cools you off when you

*need to stay warm. Give up competitive scorekeeping during athletic prac-
tice. Play not for points but for fun. Cover the timer on the treadmill and
get lost in the flow of putting one foot in front of another. Practice being, not
achieving.*

Exercise: Shadowbox

*Take the opponent out of your sport of choice. Become your own opponent.
If you lose to you, no big deal, right? Practice the moves of your skill (whether
it's sports, work, or art) all by yourself, without an audience and without
any intention toward achievement.*

Exercise: Dissolve Yourself in Teamwork

*Teamwork is team effort and shared responsibility for the outcome. As such,
any teamwork allows you a unique opportunity to hone your skills in public
without necessarily feeling like you're on the spot. Go raise a barn, join a
dragon-boat rowing crew, or just find a way to pitch in to a collective effort.
Participate to be a part of the process apart from its outcome.*

Exercise: Disown the Outcome

*Turn the products of your craft into anonymous donations. For example,
if you're a glassblower, don't bother saving every piece you make. If a piece
turns out great, keep it (display it, sell it). But if it's nothing special, own the
experience and disown the outcome. Give it away (preferably anonymously).
Keep the skill; throw away or give away the product. Keep your future free
of sentimental clutter.*

Exercise: Targetless Practice

*Shoot some balls without a hoop. Skip a pebble off the surface of a lake with
your eyes closed. Hit an invisible golf ball into nowhere. Aim and release.
Aim and release. Aim and release.*

Exercise: Comb Some Sand

*Get a Zen-style sand tray. Comb and tidy it to calm the lake of your con-
sciousness. And when the sand tray is flat, ruffle it up to remind yourself
that it was the process that calmed your mind, not the outcome.*

Exercise: Hone Your Base Skill

Any area of competence or expertise has some foundational skill(s). I call these base skills. What is the base skill or skills of the work you do to earn a living? Identify the base skill of your particular vocation and/or avocation and practice it with the aim-and-release un-self-conscious mentality. Work at it with utter oblivion to outcome when it doesn't matter, so that it flows well when it does matter.

mindfulness: the base of all bases

As always, etymology of words is a treasure trove of wisdom. The word "sport" originates from the Old French verb *desporter,* which meant "to divert, to amuse." The verb *desporter* breaks down into *des-* (away) and *porter* (to carry). That's how the word "sport" gets its original meaning of "pleasant pastime." A sport carries you (your mind) away. In its historical meaning, it's a distraction, a way to pass time, to be carried away from past-focused ruminations and future-focused preoccupations.

Nowadays, the word "sport" has acquired a connotation of competitiveness, which, when taken to an extreme, takes the "pleasant" out of the "pastime." But whichever way you slice it—whether you see sport as a pleasant pastime or a competitive pastime or whether you view your entire life as a sport or a race—one thing's clear: knowing how to step out of the fiction of the past and the future and to re-enter the present moment is an essential skill. Whether we're talking about flow, peak performance, experientially perfect performance (the way I define it), or enlightened Zen action, mindfulness is the base of all bases or, as I call it, a meta–base skill.

Exercise: Learn and Practice the Meta–Base Skill

The meta–base skill of all performance, as I see it, is this: when in action, identify with the process; when the action is over, immediately dis-identify with the outcome of your action. Once again, when acting, forget yourself; focus on the task. When you're done, dismiss any notion that this outcome is a reflection of you. Recognize that 1) you are not the outcome of the action, it's the action that is the outcome of you and 2) you have already changed: whatever you achieved or failed to achieve is nothing but an echo of what you once were. To practice this meta–base skill, pick a skill (or one of the skills) that is the base of your art or trade and engage in it. For example, if you are trying to get better at playing basketball, practice a basic throw. If you are a typist, practice the base-skill of typing. If you are a student, take a practice exam. Most arts and trades have textbooks and manuals that feature practice opportunities for the basic skills that constitute a given skill set. Go to these sources, review the appropriate knowledge base, and then select a moderate-to-high-difficulty practice opportunity. Then dive in, head-first, but without self-consciousness. While practicing, follow these basic steps:

1. *Set a goal.*

2. *Exhale any outcome preoccupation.*

3. *Inhale to enter the moment.*

4. *Merge into the behavior and identify with the action.*

5. *While going through the task or when done, dis-identify with the outcome.*

As soon as you are done and the outcome of your action crystallizes in your awareness, immediately dismiss it. Say to yourself: "I am not the outcome of this outcome," or simply "I am not this outcome." Spend some time passing time like this. Be a good sport to yourself.

conclusion: perfectionism-free performance-enhancement plan

If, in addition to overcoming your perfectionism, you are also interested in enhancing your performance, here's a mindfulness-powered, perfectionism-free, process-focused performance-enhancement plan for you to try.

Prep phase. First, practice the meta–base skill of mindfulness (in any meditational way you wish). Following this, identify the task-specific base skill pertaining to your vocation or avocation and practice engaging in this skill without any concern for the outcome (merge with the process of the action and dis-identify with the outcome of your action). Practice this task-specific base skill when you don't need it so as to be able to use it when you do need it. The goal here is to practice how to step into a task-specific moment without any undue self-consciousness and without any outcome preoccupation that might jeopardize your performance.

Application. At a make-it-or-break-it time, give yourself permission to not worry about the outcome of your effort. Recognize that you are always at your best-effort level. Perceive that failure is not an option. While you won't always be successful in others' eyes, you will always give your best effort. By giving your best in every moment, you cannot help but succeed, regardless of how that matches up with others' expectations. And remember, those expectations are moot anyway because they are not based on you. Recognize that perfect (self-un-conscious/process-focused) performance is the path to optimal performance.

Outcome recovery. Accept the result of your action as being the outcome of you, not the other way around. De-catastrophize the consequences of your performance ("It's survivable; it's not the end of the world"). Understand that even though you might have not done your all-time best, you *have* done the best you could have at that particular moment in time—which is all you could have done. Decide that your own best is enough for you, even if it's not enough for others. If you become stuck in worrying, use rumination-control skills.

CHAPTER 13

embracing the uncertainty of the future

You can strive wholeheartedly to catch the bus or get the raise, even while allowing it to be okay that you don't know whether it will happen or not.

—David Harp

As a perfectionist, you have a love-hate relationship with the future. Yes, you love the virgin, flawless, impeccable idea of it, but you also dread it because the future is fundamentally uncertain and is outside of your control. While the uncertainty of the future and uncertainty in general is a challenge for all of us, uncertainty is simply unacceptable to most perfectionists. You get anxious, worried, and even panicky when you don't know what comes next. You try to know what cannot be known. You make predictions. You seek reassurances. You overprepare. This chapter is about coping with uncertainty, about learning how to be okay with not knowing, and about recognizing the existential opportunities that come with that.

uncertainty and knowledge

Uncertainty is the lack of knowledge. But what is knowledge? Say I announce that I am going to drop a ball onto the floor. Before I actually do it, you have no knowledge of whether I'll drop it or not. Why? You cannot know the future until it has happened. An event isn't an event until it's a fact. Let's say I dropped the ball. Now, if you witnessed my doing so, you know for a fact that I dropped it. Knowledge is memory (however short-term it might be), a reporting on a fact that has already occurred.

Next I announce that I'm about to drop the ball, and I walk out of the room. You hear a thump, presumably of the ball hitting the floor. Only, you have no direct proof that I dropped the ball. The thump could have been a tapping of my heel on the floor. To know for a fact, you'd have to have direct evidence. According to the Online Etymological Dictionary, the word "evidence" is related to the Proto-Indo-European word *weid* ("vision, knowledge") and to the Latin verb *videre* ("to see, to know"). To know something for a fact, you have to witness it, to see it happen (note that the verb "to witness" is also related to the word *weid*). After all, to see *is* to know.

now sets the ceiling on certainty

The present time sets the limit on what can be known. Paranormal claims aside, we cannot see what doesn't exist (the future). This present time, this now, is the event horizon of your knowledge. Certainty cannot extend any further into the future than this present moment. Beyond this now is terra incognita.

Not Knowing Is Part of Being In Time

Regardless of how far we can travel into the speculative future in our minds, our bodies are never any farther than the present moment. Imagine that you announce with great certainty that you are about to drop the ball on the floor. You'd know, right? Not really. Even *your* certainty is illusory. There is a chance (however unlikely it may be) that your hand simply won't open for whatever reason. A fact isn't a fact until it's a fact. Not knowing the future is an inevitable and, therefore, normal part of being in time.

Exercise: Face the Wall of Uncertainty

Go up to a wall. Stand right against it, with your nose touching it. Meditate on this: this wall represents this moment. You can tell what's on this side of the wall (in the present and in the recent past), but you have no way of knowing what's behind it (in the future). That's how it is now and that's how it's always been. Recognize that you are always against the invisible wall of uncertainty. No need to beat your head against this fact. Accept the inevitability of uncertainty. What you know ends here and now. Face the wall of the unknown. Recognize that no one, not a single mind that is alive, is a step ahead of you. All six-plus billion of us are standing with our noses flat against this same wall of the unknown. No one's behind, and no one's ahead. We are all here, now. No one's on the other side of this wall to tell you what's in the next moment. All of us—even experts, prophets, visionaries, statisticians, psychics, seers, sorcerers, diviners, astrologists, and "theory of everything" physicists—are on this side of the wall of uncertainty.

the next best thing to knowing

So, what are we to do if we can't know? In the absence of certainty, we create pseudo-certainty by formulating beliefs and assumptions. Believing isn't knowing, but it's the next best thing. Say you and I make plans to meet. Neither of us knows with certainty whether the meeting will take place, but we assume that it will, and we operate under this assumption.

Belief Isn't Knowledge, but It Feels Just the Same

Belief is a surrogate for knowledge. If we don't know something, we develop beliefs. Beliefs serve as pseudo-knowledge. As such, they guide our behavior the same way as knowledge would. A belief is when you act as if you know, even though you actually don't. A case in point: most people who will die in their sleep will go to bed that final night believing and assuming that they'll wake up the next morning, as always. They will act *as if they know* that they will wake up, even though they don't. That's emotionally useful. Imagine the turmoil you'd feel every night if you didn't make this assumption!

illusions of certainty

We try to reduce uncertainty in our lives by relying on promises, guidance, and controlling behaviors.

Promises Can't Guarantee the Future

A promise is a statement of intent, not a guarantee. If I tell you that I'll be there (at some particular place and time) or that I'll be there for you (as a friend), this future I'm talking about isn't here yet. No one can guarantee a particular version of the future because it hasn't happened yet. So what do you really know when you have secured a promise from me? Only that I said what I said. You can choose to believe that I meant it, but that doesn't mean that you know that I'll follow through with my promise. Even I don't know that. Sure, I might sincerely *believe* that I will. But I, like you, am too close to the wall of the unknown. Who knows what might happen, how we'll all change in time? Recognize that knowledge cannot be taken on faith.

Others' Guidance Is Others' Guesswork

As a perfectionist, you try to avoid mistakes, and when unsure, you might seek out guidance. But guidance is guesswork. No one knows with certainty what's going to happen next. Nor is there a protocol or a set of rules that can predict the future with certainty. Protocols tell you about what worked in the past, not about what will work in the future. No protocol can envision (know) with 100 percent certainty the future that doesn't yet exist. How can there be foolproof guidance in a universe that is always changing?

Pretensions of Control

As a perfectionist, you don't like delegating. By doing everything yourself, you are trying to control the future. If you're solely in charge of a task, everything will be just the way you envisioned, right? Wrong. You only get an illusion of control. No matter how much you try to control the controllable, the future, by its very essence, is beyond your control. How can you control what doesn't yet exist? On some level, you already know this. And that's why you might have routines, rituals, and even superstitions that give you an illusion of control, a belief that if you do such and such, you can assure a certain future outcome. Face it: you can't. What you can control is your reaction to being out of control.

Exercise: A Balancing Act, Part 1

Try to balance a pen on your index finger. Give it a few minutes. We'll continue with this exercise in a moment.

Exercise: A Balancing Act, Part 2

My guess is that the pen immediately fell off the tip of your finger each time you tried. With this information in mind, what's your prediction of what will happen the next time you try? That the pen will fall? Most likely. You don't know it for a fact, but your life experience and your intuitive understanding of physics tell you so. So let's just accept it and have fun with it. Let's turn this seemingly impossible balancing act into an opportunity to practice being balanced about not being in control.

Position the pen on the tip of your index finger and immediately, without hesitation, let it fall. Why fight your own predictions? Try this ten times and have fun as you let go of trying to control the uncontrollable.

Uncertainty Is (Almost) Like Gravity

When we were toddlers, we all had a problem with gravity. We fell and scratched our knees or bumped our noggins. But we came to accept gravity as an ever-present parameter of our physical world. Same with uncertainty: uncertainty is an ever-present parameter of our temporal and psychological world. That's the inescapable gravity of uncertainty. However, there is one caveat: as seemingly certain as gravity is, its certainty is provisional. Gravity is a function of a certain arrangement of physical variables. If this arrangement were to be changed, gravity might cease to operate. Uncertainty of the future, however, is a basic fact of reality. There never will be a time when we can know what hasn't happened yet. As long as there is a future ahead of us, it will always remain an unknown. Do I know that for a fact? Of course not. But I believe this as if I knew it for a fact. What else is there to do?

You Already Know How Not to Know

So, there are two choices you have for dealing with the uncontrollable. You can try to control it, which is an anxiety-fraught delusion. Or you can try to control your reaction to the uncontrollable, which can be acceptance, courage, and possibly a sense of fun. Our whole life is made of assumptions: that the alarm clock will work, that the car will start, that the coffee cup will be there when we reach for it without looking at it. We already know how not to know. And we're damned good at it.

Exercise: The Art of Emotionally Pragmatic Assumption

Do you know that your car will start tomorrow morning as you head out to work? Of course not. So how come you're not worried? If your car doesn't start, it might throw off your whole day. Heck, you might lose your job over it! And yet, here you are, reading this, not worried at all. What's the trick?

When faced with the uncertainty of the unknown, we have a choice to drive blind into the unknown or to turn on the halogen headlamp of reassuring hypothesizing. Hypothesizing about what will happen is entirely natural. There's absolutely nothing wrong with having beliefs in the absence of knowledge. Since we don't know either way (if the car will start or not), we might as well assume that it will. An emotionally pragmatic assumption is a belief that you can live with, a belief that helps you survive uncertainty with the minimum of distress.

In formulating an emotionally pragmatic assumption, it's important not to let an assumption become an entitled presumption. Both an assumption and a presumption are ways of dealing with the unknown. To assume is to suppose that something is, was, or will be the case without evidence or proof. To presume is to take for granted that something is, was, or will be the case. Thus, an assumption is a tentative hypothesis and a presumption is an inflexible expectation.

In the weeks to come, practice conscious assuming without presuming. When faced with some crucial unknown, allow yourself to formulate an emotionally pragmatic assumption without letting it become an inflexible expectation. Recognize that just because you have a preference for a certain version of the future, that doesn't mean reality will comply. Reality owes us nothing. For example, think: "Since I don't know either way, this is what I've chosen to assume. Assuming this will help me feel less nervous as I wait to see what actually happens. In making this assumption, I realize that I am merely expressing a hopeful hypothesis. I am not entitled to any certain version of the future. The future is outside of my control and I accept that." Assume, but don't presume.

Exercise: Uncertainty U.

You've been here before: wanting to know something, not knowing it, and having to wait to find out. Your whole life you've been studying at Uncertainty University. Now, review the pivotal, make-it-or-break-it moments (or periods) of uncertainty that you've survived. Remind yourself of your success in dealing with the unknown. Recall how you dealt with that. Remember what you thought to tone down the worry, how you soothed yourself, how you survived one moment of not knowing after another. If you are alive, you're a survivor of uncertainty. So next time, when uncertain again about something crucial, toss that graduation cap up in the air, once again defying the gravity of not knowing with an emotionally pragmatic assumption.

Clinging to Certainty Comes at the Cost of Mindlessness

Every day we mindlessly formulate and renew hundreds of micro-assumptions. I invite you to recognize that, when it comes to the future, you are and have always been operating on beliefs, not knowledge. Instead of mindlessly projecting high beams of self-reassuring assumptions, let us now and then have the courage to drive with the lights off. Let us at least once unambiguously acknowledge that we are moving into the unknown. We can open our minds to this inevitable great doubt of living and experience the awe of this experiment that we call life. And let us also realize that unless we occasionally take off the blinders of our assumptions about what will be, we'll be unable to see what is.

We are afraid of what we don't know. So we hide in the knowledge of the past and in beliefs about the future. As we cling to our memory and imagination, we ignore what is. We fail to see that reality, like a wheel, keeps turning, renewing itself in its entirety with every spin. Instead of rereading the same old reassuring postcards of reminiscence that we send ourselves from the past into the present, instead of confusing what is with what was or with what should be, I invite you to open your eyes to face the fact that we are traveling blind, on faith, not on knowledge. Know that! Own the illusion of belief. Accept the uncertainty as an inevitable part of the human condition.

Exercise: Acknowledge that You Don't Know

Having anticipated all you could anticipate, having prepared yourself for every possible reasonable contingency, face the fact that you still don't know a thing about what happens next. As sure as you are, as reassured as you have been by "experts," you cannot know what doesn't exist. Acknowledge it to yourself. Exercise the courage of living. Now and then, turn the halogen lights of hypothesizing off and drive blindly into the unknown. Think: "Sure, I have all kinds of ideas and assumptions I could make, but this time I will allow myself to simply not know. Fact is, I don't know what will happen, and I am okay with this because that's normal. That's how it's always been, is, and will be. That much I know."

Exercise: Accept Uncertainty, Treasure the Present

For a moment, assume that there won't be a tomorrow. Recognize that by accepting the uncertainty that there will be a future, you invite a degree of mindful presence into your life. Allow yourself to treasure the present moment rather than taking it for granted. Most of us expect the next moment to roll around as though it were guaranteed. It's not. Instead of hiding from uncertainty in beliefs and assumptions about how the future should be, take refuge in the present and notice what still is. Try living in the moment as if it were the last. Open up to the urgent poignancy of the present.

conclusion: reframe the uncertainty

Recognize that uncertainty is the prerequisite for surprise. It is the future, not the present or the past, that is the source of all news and novelty. Look the future in the eye with eager curiosity: see the amazing possibilities that you won't find anywhere else in time!

beyond certainty: cultivating the don't-know mind

Once established, the categories become permanent.

—Edward de Bono

*The greater the doubt, the greater the awakening;
the smaller the doubt, the smaller the awakening.
No doubt, no awakening.*

—C. C. Chang

In the preceding chapter we examined the challenges of uncertainty. Well, certainty can be as paralyzing as uncertainty. As a
perfectionist, you defend against the uncertainty of the future with
the certainty of your past and present. You develop inflexible and
at times superstitious rituals, habits, rules, routines, and protocols
designed to somehow keep the not-yet-existent future reality in
control. Barricaded behind these self-reassurances, you box yourself in. Certainty becomes a prison. In fear of losing control, you
become controlling. Your creativity becomes hostage to your habits.
Your spontaneity withers as you keep defaulting to the already
trodden paths. You close your mind to outside input. You become
the expert. You become deaf to feedback and correction. Eventually
your rules, routines, habits, and protocols begin to fail you as you
grow more and more out of touch. You fall back on what you know.
You become ever more rigid and uncompromising in a stifling cen-
trifuge of self-referencing certainty. This is the unfortunate trajectory of perfectionism: from lofty ambition to cynical stagnation,
from enthusiasm to bitterness, from being a rising star to becoming
a perfectionistic burnout. As the perfectionistic mind closes, life
shrinks. In this chapter we examine the perils of certainty and work
toward cultivating an open mind (also known as *beginner's mind*, or
don't-know mind).

the impasse of certainty

As a perfectionist, you like being "right" and doing the "right" thing.
This emphasis on being right can lead to dogma. Certainty is rigidity. Doubt is tentativeness. A mind that is certain is a closed mind.
A mind that is in doubt is an open mind. When a mind is uncertain it searches for knowledge. A mind full of certainty is full of
memory: it knows what it knows and needs to know nothing else.
Such a mind is asleep, not interested in what is, only in confirming
what was. Thus, certainty is mindlessness. Ellen J. Langer wrote:
"mindlessness is the rigid reliance on old categories" whereas mindfulness is "the continual creation of new ones" (1989, 63). If I start
watching a movie and I don't like the first ten minutes of it, I might

categorize it as a movie I don't like and stop watching it. If, however, I remain open minded and continue to watch it, I might discover that I do, after all, like the movie and will recategorize it. Certainty is a foreclosure on the ever-coming flow of information. It's the end of analysis, the presumption that reality will remain in the future what it is at the moment. But reality is, of course, changing every moment and creating new information. If you are not creating new categories, you're missing new information. As a perfectionist, you tend to be certain beyond doubt about your version of what's right. Certainty becomes a disability. After all, how can you learn something new without being willing to revise your old categories? How can you revise your old categories if you are dead certain that they are right? And how can you let go of your certainty if you're afraid of not knowing? You can't, unless you cultivate a don't-know mind.

Certainty Blocks Creativity

In addition to inhibiting learning, certainty can also stand in the way of your creativity and playfulness. Langer explains that creating and recreating categories is at the heart of recreation (as in playing), and the reluctance to do so tends "to deaden a playful approach" (1989, 64). Indeed, if we respond to new stimuli as if they were old stimuli, the new is no longer novel enough to be stimulating. Edward de Bono explains that "the mind is a cliché-making and cliché-using system" (1990, 38). A cliché view of the world ignores the ever-renewing suchness of the present. While clichés and stereotypes give us a comforting illusion of familiarity, we end up getting shortchanged on what's new. Just as much as a human mind needs the comfort of its clichés, stereotypes, and patterns, it needs stimulation and renewal.

nurturing the don't-know mind

Buddhist psychology values not knowing and offers a training method that is particularly useful for cultivating tolerance of uncertainty. This method is called *koan training*. When we ask a question that can be answered, we limit the scope of inquiry to the information that can fit into old categories. By pondering a question that cannot be answered in principal, we open the mind to its limitations and challenge it to go beyond what it knows. In so doing, the mind is freed from itself; it breaks away from the categories that stand in the way between what it knows and what is. As such, koans shut off dualistic logic and dull the linguistic scissors of dichotomy with which we define and cut up the wholeness of reality.

Koan Learning: Addition by Subtraction

Koans have been described as "quests for non-answers" (James Austin, 1999, 110), or as questions "with no rational answer" (David Harp, 1999, 107). They have also been defined as "pithy, epigrammatic, elusive utterances that seem to have a psychotherapeutic effect in liberating practitioners from bondage to ignorance" (Heine and Wright, 2000, 3). While unanswerable, koan questions serve to liberate from the arrogance of certainty. By cultivating a don't-know mind, you add to your knowledge base by subtracting the arrogance of certainty.

Uncertainty Training Therapy

Psychologically speaking, koans are a unique way to inoculate a human mind against the anxiety of uncertainty. When we encounter uncertainty, we are stumped. Uncertainty frustrates us with its enigmatic nonsense. Koans, in their unanswerable quality, effectively simulate such moments of uncertainty. Author Hee-Jin Kim explains: the koans are "realized, not solved" (2000, 295). Admittedly, this explanation is a bit of a puzzle itself. But here's how I make sense of it. A koan, once again, is an unanswerable puzzle. If we take it on, we begin banging our head against the wall of the unknown. At some point, we realize that there is no solution, and we settle into a don't-know mind. This realization, of course, comes up pretty early in the koan work. And it serves as the true beginning, not the end of the process. Knowing in advance that you are working with an unanswerable question, you accept your limitations. No longer trying to know the unknowable, you calmly remain with the question in a state of not knowing. Knowingly, you keep chasing the tail of not knowing in a process that, I believe, very much parallels the day-to-day mystery of life—thus, the potential therapeutic value of koan work as a kind of one-question-therapy that can help soothe the perfectionistic thirst for answers.

Exercise: Perfectionism-Specific Koans

If you were hungry (for approval, control, or reflection), and a koan were a can of ego-food, you wouldn't be able to open it. But see if you can. I've devised the following set of koans with perfectionism in mind. Spend a day or two on each.

- *Show me your value. For example: "show me your value" is me asking you to show me "your value." As you work on this koan, as you keep recycling it through your mind, the phrase will boil down to a koan-stem phrase such as "show value" or "show my value." Let this thought percolate until you feel you have a valuable insight. Repeat with other koans.*

- *Show me a shouldn't.*

- *How would you describe perfection without words?*

- *What happens to reality when it's gone?*

- *What color is approval?*

- *What is your mind full of when you are a success?*

- *What is your mind full of when you are a failure?*

- *When does a fact become fiction?*

- *Perfect the echo.*

- *How much would you pay for a pound of certainty?*

- *How do you add to what is?*

- *How perfect are you when you sleep?*

- *Show me a different you right now.*

- *Add to the past.*

- *Subtract from the present.*

- *How's your (my) potential doing?*

- *When you think "Not good enough," who thinks that?*

- *Would you rather be perfect or breathe?*

- *What word do you want to be?*

- *What's the square root of perfection?*

- *If perfection were a question, what would be the answer?*

- *If perfection were a blank waist belt, where should I poke a hole?*

- *Who appraises the appraiser?*

Exercise: Practice Syadvada Tentativeness

Syadvada is a practice of tentativeness in expression that is associated with the ancient Jain tradition of India (Radhakrishnan and Moore 1957). In Sanskrit, the word syad means "perhaps" or "maybe" or "in some ways." The Syadvada system consists of a total of seven propositions that were designed specifically to counteract dogmatic thinking when attempting to describe the multifaceted complexity of reality. Practice the following three as a way of infusing a degree of tactful tentativeness when you find yourself at odds with someone's opinion. These three propositions are:

1. *In some ways, it is.*

2. *In some ways, it is not.*

3. *In some ways, it is and it is not.*

When encountering a point of view that you disagree with, practice responding with any of these statements. For example, say you say something I disagree with. Instead of firing back that "You're dead wrong," I communicate my disagreement with the help of Syadvada-style tentativeness: "in some ways what you say is so" or "in some ways what you say is so and in some ways it isn't." Use Syadvada-style phrasing to keep the channels of communication open and to tone down the unattractive definitiveness of certainty.

conclusion: have a sip of not knowing

In closing the chapter, let me offer you a classic Buddhist anecdote that extols the virtue of not knowing, as retold by David Harp: A scientist visited a Buddhist to learn about Buddhism from a "scientific" point of view. "Before beginning, the Buddhist suggested having tea. He filled the scientist's teacup to the brim, paused for a second, then poured more tea into the cup. The scientist leaped up as the hot tea cascaded into his lap. 'A teacup that is too full,' the Buddhist said, 'can receive nothing additional. Neither can a mind'" (1999, 107).

PART 6

coexistence, compassion, connection

While this part is of relevance for all types of perfectionists, it is of particular importance for control-hungry perfectionists, other-directed (outwardly focused) perfectionists, and those perfectionists who struggle with anger.

CHAPTER 15

from social vacuum to compassionate coexistence

Comprendre, c'est pardoner. (To understand is to forgive.)

—Madame de Staël

We differ from others only in what we do and don't do—not in what we are.

—Anthony de Mello

Perfectionists aren't only hard on themselves. They also tend to be quite critical and judgmental of others. This kind of other-focused perfectionism is like running with scissors. Armed with dichotomies (of right/wrong, perfect/imperfect, good/bad), you dissect the world into us and them, then further reduce the subset of us into us and them. As a result, your circle of connections shrinks: the higher the standards you have for others, the harder it is for others to meet them; the harder it is for others to meet them, the easier it is for you to reject others. And the more you reject others, the more you feel rejected by them. It's a vicious loop with a tightening diameter, a social noose of sorts. This final chapter is about forgiveness, compassion, and coexistence with others' imperfections.

forgiveness isn't just letting go or moving on

There are many approaches to forgiveness. Some people think that you *should* forgive. I don't think so: forgiveness is not a matter of obligation. "Have to"-style forgiveness is meaningless. Some people extol the virtues of forgiveness, saying that it's good for you because it allows you to move on. True, but this kind of moving on isn't really forgiveness—it's just an attempt to put something out of your mind without any resolution. This kind of hedonistic letting go is glorified rumination control. So then what is forgiveness? How does it work?

Exercise: Define Forgiveness

Assuming you're willing to forgive, how would you go about it? Ponder the mechanism of forgiveness. Ask yourself: what would I have to think to be able to forgive the offender? Think about the times when you've received forgiveness. Try to recall what it was like. Did it feel like a formality? Did you feel like they (whoever they were) were just saying it? Did you believe it? What convinced you that they really forgave you? What maintained your doubt? What were you told? In sum, ponder the times you forgave and the times you were forgiven and see if you can distill the essence of forgiveness.

forgiveness is identification

Here's my take on it. *To forgive, you have to identify with another's imperfection.* Put differently, you have to see the perfection behind the imperfection; you have to recognize that the person who infringed on your well-being did the best he or she could at that given point in time, given his or her abilities and limitations. This kind of forgiveness requires true understanding of the other person (which is a lot of work) and a history of self-acceptance. Indeed, to forgive others for their imperfections, we first have to learn to forgive our own imperfections by realizing that at any given point we are doing our best. To identify with another's imperfection means realizing that the person was all he or she could be at a given moment in time. It means understanding that if he or she could have been any more moral, any more mature, any more ethical, any more mindful, any more motivated, any better at problem solving, any better at emotional self-regulation, any wiser, any smarter, any less defensive (and so on), then that's what would have happened. To forgive, we have to understand that the offender had to be what he or she was at the moment of the offense. And that's a very tall order indeed!

That's why you find this chapter at the end of this book. I'm hoping that by now you're better able to accept yourself just as you are, which puts you in a position to identify with others just as they are. What starts with self-acceptance ends with the acceptance of others.

Let me clarify. You don't have to forgive; you certainly don't have to really forgive. You can just say that you forgive, not mean it, get the person in question out of your way, and move on. There's nothing wrong with that. If somebody trespassed on your well-being, you don't owe them forgiveness. Let me reiterate this loudly and clearly: I don't believe in spiritually mandatory forgiveness. That's pro-forma, superficial, meaningless forgiveness. For forgiveness to be authentic, it has to be a choice, it has to be an expression of preference. So, if for some personal reason you decided that you mean to forgive, if you feel that you *want* to forgive, then the work's cut out for you. And here are some of the obstacles that you might find on the way.

obstacle: categorical and dichotomous thinking

To judge, we need categories. To forgive, we have to go beyond our categories—we have to examine the reality of what happened through somebody else's categories. As a perfectionist, you tend to be more categorical than others. You like your categories. You don't like to revise them, let alone look at the world through somebody else's lens (categories, perspective). Plus, your categories tend to be polarized (thanks to dichotomous, all-or-nothing, black-and-white thinking). Thus, your inability to forgive is based on ignoring what is in favor of what should be. Put differently, the inability to forgive is the insistence that whatever is shouldn't be. Furthermore, this inability to forgive is the inability to accept that your shoulds aren't everyone else's shoulds.

Everyone has their own shoulds. We are often appalled by how unapologetic somebody else might feel after they have (in our opinion) trespassed on our well-being. As we reel from their offensiveness, we find it particularly unforgivable that they aren't sorry. In order to be able to forgive the offending party's lack of remorse, we have to once again examine the situation from their perspective. We have to walk away from our shoulds and examine the shoulds that determined their thinking and their course of action. When we're able to understand where they're coming from, we are in a better place to identify with them. We can then think: "Well, if I were like you, I'd be thinking the way you were thinking, and then I'd do what you did. Seeing your mental software, your worldview, knowing the shoulds that guide your reflexes, I can now relate to what you did. I can understand that what I see as an unforgivable imperfection, you see as a perfectly normal course of action. That makes all the difference."

Exercise: Forgiveness Is Perspective Taking

As the French say, to understand is to forgive. To forgive, we have to learn to see past our own nose. Sit down and look straight in front of you. Now turn your head to your right, over your right shoulder. Try to see what's behind you. Now close your right eye and notice how doing so dramatically reduces your field of vision. Open and close your right eye several times, and notice what happens to the transparency of your nose. When your right eye is closed, you see the left side of your nose very distinctly. Your nose is blocking your field of vision. When you open your right eye, all of a sudden your nose becomes somewhat transparent. You see it and you see through it. Even though your left eye is staring at the same technically nontranspar-ent left side of your nose, when both of your eyes are open at the same time, the barrier that had blocked your field of view is much more transparent. Why? Because you see more when you see from more than one point of view. If you are motivated to forgive another person, you have to start with under-standing their point of view. To understand someone else, you have to allow yourself to see through their point of view. That is perspective taking.

understanding the story of what is

Gaining understanding in order to forgive is more than just changing your perspective, more than just seeing the event through another person's eyes. In order to forgive, you also have to understand why what happened *had* to happen. "The future enters into us long before it happens," says Rainer Maria Rilke (1986, 84). Understanding the inevitability of what happened helps us see that the transgressor, too, was a victim of history. Thus, forgiveness depends on your rec-ognition of the fact that the other person, just like you, is perfectly imperfect. That person is doing his best at any given point in time (no matter how deviant that best might be in comparison to your expectations or in comparison to social and cultural norms).

Motive Focus

The pursuit of well-being is the core motivation, and there are a plethora of ways in which we try to find well-being. Some people seek their well-being by going to work; others may boost your lawn mower for money to buy drugs. Motivationally, there is no difference. Let's say you busted the lawn-mower thief red-handed. Imagine that you ask him what he's doing on your property, and, in a rare moment of candor, he explains that he wanted to steal your lawn mower. That's a goal, not a motive. To get to his core motivation, you have to keep on asking questions.

> *You:* Why did you want to steal from me?
>
> *Thief:* I needed money.
>
> *You:* Why did you need the money?
>
> *Thief:* I needed to get high.
>
> *You:* Why did you need to get high?
>
> *Thief:* I didn't want to feel sick, (or) I wanted to feel good.

Now, there's your core motive: not wanting to feel sick or wanting to feel good is the pursuit of well-being. So, the difference isn't in the "why" but in the "how" we go about meeting our needs and desires. No one's motivationally evil. Motivationally, everyone's innocent. It's just that some of us are less sophisticated (more limited) than others in their modus operandi. Why? That's the history that has to be understood in each case. To forgive, you have to see beyond the behavior. You have to be willing to hear the whole story and to unravel the determinism of the other person's actions to see the inevitability of what happened. Only then you will be able to see the event from their point of view, identifying with them and, thus, enabling yourself to forgive.

Exercise: Serial-Why to Forgiveness

Review the serial-why method of self-forgiveness (chapter 7) and practice applying it to others' behaviors. This technique will help you forgive others for behavior that infringes on your well-being. For example, let's say that a coworker is having a problem with a copier. You offer to help, but your assistance is irritably rejected. You fume: "I was just trying to be nice. Why did he have to be so rude?" Don't just leave the rhetorical question hanging in your mind. Answer it. Put on your serial-why hat and speculate: Perhaps he was frustrated with himself for not being able to troubleshoot the problem on his own. But why did he have to be so rude? Why couldn't he just politely decline my offer of help? Why did he have to displace his frustration onto me when I was just trying to help? Maybe because he lacks psychological savvy or self-awareness. Or perhaps because he doesn't know how to manage his anger or felt embarrassed. But why couldn't he manage his anger better? Why did he have to become so frustrated with himself for something as trivial as not knowing how to operate a Xerox? Who knows; perhaps he grew up with a hypercritical parent and is therefore perfectionistically hard on himself. Does this sound like something you could identify with? If you can identify with that, then do. Spend some time thinking of recent slights and offenses against you and practice unraveling the determinism behind those moments to identify and forgive.

from identifying with one to identifying with all

While you might not be able to unravel the mystery of why so-and-so did such and such in each specific case, there are two key things that you share in common with the "transgressor":

- The other's motive is the same as yours—the pursuit of well-being (and that's something you can identify with).

- The other person, just like you, is doing the best that he or she can at any given point in time, given his or her level of psychological sophistication, insight, problem-solving skills, and coping. In other words, just like you, the other person is perfectly imperfect (and that's something else you can identify with).

By being mindful of these common denominators, you can begin to cultivate a willingness to identify with others. This identification will serve as a platform for universal compassion.

Exercise: Extending the Range of Your Compassion

Think of a heinous act or crime you've heard about. First, do the prep work. Research the backstory. If there is a book about what happened, read it. If there is a movie about it, watch it. As you study the facts of the case and the person responsible, make a mental note of things you can relate to.

Now, having researched the whole story of the person behind the crime, imagine that you had been born with that person's exact genetic makeup. Imagine that your brain and body were identical to that person's. In other words, imagine that you thought like them and looked like them and acted (physically) like them. Imagine that you had been exposed to the exact same ideas, the same parenting, the same social modeling or lack thereof, and the same environmental influences as those in that person's life. In other words, imagine that you shared the same exact interplay of nature and nurture as that person and, as a result, that you shared the same experiences and history as they did. If you can imagine that, then you can imagine yourself doing the heinous act that they did. If you were physically and psychologically set up just like that person and had been placed at the same historical coordinate of circumstances, you would have ended up with the same domino effect. You might object: "I would have made a different choice." Yes, the you that exists now, the you that is a function of a very different life, would have made a different choice. Recognize that your choices reflect your life story. Understand that you wouldn't be the you you are now if you had been born with that person's genetics and raised under the same social influences. You would be that person, not this person. Imagine that! Imagine, identify, relate, and forgive.

Exercise: Find the Unforgivable and Forgive It

What can't you forgive? Somebody cutting in front of you in traffic? Are you sure you can't identify with that? How about someone who's lost their temper? If you've ever lost your temper, I'm sure you can identify with that and therefore forgive it. What are your pet peeves? What angers, annoys, and bugs the hell out of you? Catalog all the slights, offenses, inefficiencies, imperfections, and insecurities that get under your skin. What offends your sensitivities? What do you find unforgivable in others? Then see if you can identify with any of those things. If you can, go ahead and try to forgive them. Think of some specific examples of actions that have wounded you physically, psychologically, and/or financially. Challenge yourself to see the humanity behind the offense. Document your conclusions.

factor in the context

The willingness to forgive is dependent on your explanatory style. Let's say you are in a meeting with a coworker. After the meeting is over, you observe that coworker forcefully shut the door as she leaves the conference room. Without a moment's delay, you search for an explanation. And in doing so, you are limited to two types of explanations: you can attribute the event either to a force within the person or to a force outside of the person. The former, the *personal explanation,* holds a person accountable for a given event: She did it. She slammed the door. The latter, the *contextual explanation,* takes the context (the situational/environmental factors) into account: She didn't do it. A strong draft caused the door to slam shut. If you attribute the event to personal factors, you take what happened personally. If, on the other hand, you speculate that it was the context that was responsible, not the person, then you wouldn't take her action personally. Naturally, the fewer things you take personally, the fewer there are to forgive.

The Benefit of the Doubt

Giving someone the benefit of the doubt is an empty cliché unless you have an actual blueprint for how to do it. Contextual explanation is the way to go. By considering the possibility that someone's actions might be influenced by the circumstances (environment, context, situation), you put in doubt any notion that the person meant to offend you. Then you each win: the other person benefits from your nonpersonalizing view of the situation, and you benefit by not feeling that what happened was meant as a personal affront to you.

Exercise: Become a Benefactor

Become a benefactor. Give out the benefit of the doubt like candy on Halloween. I know it's a bit scary: strangers knock on the doors of your life, the innocence of their motives masked by the seeming callousness of their behaviors. Doubt your knee-jerk thought that their unpleasant actions are personal. Instead, think: "It's the context, not the person." Give the other person the benefit of your doubt and receive the benefit of being able to put the issue to rest.

factor in the context of personality

Note that the word "context" is to be understood not just as the immediate situation, but also as the psychology of the specific person. Case in point: think of some people you know pretty well. Now and then they might do something that you used to take personally, but now you know better and no longer take offense. "That's just how they are," you explain to a friend who doesn't know them.

Let's go back to the vignette with the door slam. Let's say there was no draft that could have slammed the door. But context still played a role. The contextual element you still need to consider is your coworker's personality. Yes, she slammed the door, and technically you could nail her for it. Or you can forgive her by recognizing the context of her personality: "That's just how she is. She has trouble accepting feedback, no matter whom it comes from. It's not personal." Merab Mamardashvilli, an iconoclastic Soviet Georgian philosopher, expressed this idea as follows: "Now I can only be what I am now because I cannot cancel the moment that precedes this moment" (2000, 374). Mamardashvilli suggests that the way you are now is a circumstance that cannot be canceled. This "now" version of you is the reality of the present and it cannot be otherwise. You, the way you are right now, *is* the very context (circumstance) that you act in accordance with. He concludes: "I will be different when the circumstance is different" (ibid.). In other words, I will be different when I am different. On some level, this sounds like an excuse. But there is a way in which it's a legitimate explanation. Indeed, if I am aware and mindful of how I am and if I know how I want to be in the next moment, then perhaps I will be able to be different in the next moment. But if I am neither mindful of how I am nor motivated or equipped to change, then the way I am now will probably survive into yet another moment and I will remain the same. My self-awareness, my motivation to change, my ability to change— all these variables of change are also part of my current personal circumstance.

Whether you see this perspective as an excuse or as an explanation is part of your circumstance as well. If you're not ready to see it as a legitimate explanation and use it as a launch-pad for compassion, then that's that. You're as willing to forgive as you are. If you could be any more forgiving at this point in time, then you would be. Whichever way we slice it, I encourage you to recognize that personality is the echo of a person's historical context. Factor it in if you're looking for access to forgiveness.

forgive and forget?
forget about forgetting

Forgiving has nothing to do with forgetting. While we can forgive on demand (by identifying with others' imperfection), we cannot forget on demand. Memory just doesn't work that way. By equating forgiveness with forgetting you run the risk of not being able to forgive. Because when you try to "forgive and forget," every time your brain wanders over to that past event, you end up feeling like a compassion failure. So forget about needing to forget. Just remember to forgive.

forgive and encourage change

Compassion and forgiveness are not a get-out-of-jail-free card. When someone transgresses against us, it certainly makes sense for us to protect ourselves against being victimized in the future. When one person's behavior puts another person's well-being in danger and appears to be at risk for recidivism, we would be wise to do more than forgive. It behooves us to insist on some kind of rehabilitation process in order to reduce the chance of re-offense. If we can insist on change, if we can somehow encourage it psychologically or incentivize it legally or financially, we should. If we can't, then we can't. Such is life.

identifying with the core self

Each time you choose not to forgive, you dis-identify with the rest of humanity one person at a time. If you find yourself in a kind of emotional vacuum, here's the last chance for escape back into the world of connections. Instead of trying to identify with others on the basis of similarity, identify with them on the basis of sameness.

Recognize that what stands between you and others is your mind, the information in your head. While everyone's mind is different, you can certainly build connections on the basis of similarity of what you think and what the other person thinks. This is a connection at a mind level, at the level of information. This kind of connection doesn't last because minds are always changing. Furthermore, you yourself are not your mind—you are the consciousness behind it. The same goes for the other person: they too are not what they think, feel, sense, or do. They, like you, are the consciousness that exists before, during, and after those thoughts, feelings, and behaviors. Trying to identify on the basis of what we are not is like trying to build a bridge in the air. When you find your perfect other half, initially the connection's strong. But, before you know it, your perfectionistic mind finds ways in which your "better half" can be... better. And so goes that connection of similarity.

So, why not identify on the basis of sameness, not similarity? Why not connect to the other through the sameness of the core self that we seem to share? Why not identify on the basis of consciousness, on the basis of that primordial awareness that we all have in common? Why not identify on the basis of *oneness*? After all, oneness means zero degrees of separation. Forgiveness is a recognition that, in essence, we are all the same.

Exercise: Am-ness as a Basis for Identification, Forgiveness, and Connection

In chapter 10, we explored exercises that help you experience am-ness. Go back and review those exercises now. But this time, recognize that at the moment you experience am-ness, there is no essential difference between you and the other—just informational difference. In other words, break the state of am-ness with the thought: "I am you/he/she/they." Or, if you're trying to apply this technique to a specific case of offense, break the state of am-ness with the thought: "What I am between my thoughts is the same as what the offender is between their thoughts. At core, we are the same. At the level of consciousness, we are the same. We are different only in terms of information, in terms of thoughts, feelings, and sensations that pass through us. But neither I nor that person is the information, neither I nor he/she is the thoughts, feelings, or sensations that pass through us." More specifically, identify the person you wish to forgive. Next, tap into that gap in between the thoughts, into that state of pure am-ness. Finally, break it with the thought of identification: "I am he/she. At core, I am the same. Minds (thoughts, feelings, memories, information) aside, we are one."

Exercise: Water Is Water

Get two bottles of water and a marker. Label one bottle "I" and the other bottle "You." Pour a couple of spoonfuls of sugar into the I bottle and a couple of spoonfuls of salt into the You bottle. Shake both bottles. Put them down. Watch the sugar and salt swirl. Notice the differences between the two bottles. Wait until the sugar and salt dissolve. While sugar water looks more transparent than saltwater, recognize that the water itself hasn't changed. Water is water. You can distill it back to its original state from either of these two solutions.

Consider sugar and salt here as symbols of information. You are full of "this" and I am full of "that." The difference between you and me is this or that. But if we dissolve our minds down to their essence, to their base, what remains is the same—the pure water of awareness. What you are in between your thoughts and what I am in between my thoughts are indistinguishable. Without any information to distinguish one mind from another, all consciousness is the same. Space is space, whatever you clutter it with.

When struggling to forgive, we try to put ourselves into somebody else's mind. But the other's experience just doesn't taste quite right: we feel that under the same circumstances we'd be different. The salt of forgiveness is to understand that if you and I were informationally the same, there'd be no difference in the taste, and we would do the same thing. To forgive, you have to understand that. Spend enough time in the other's perspective to see past the informational differences, to clearly see the sameness of intentions (pursuit of well-being) and the person-specific perfection of the attempts.

self-acceptance = other-acceptance

1.

We confuse perfection with imperfection

But there is no difference

Unless, of course, we compare *what is* with *what isn't.*

2.

If we could be right this very moment better, worse or other than what we are right now

We wouldn't be ourselves.

But we are, *perfectly imperfect.*

3.

It is always like that, not just during *this* now

But *at any now* that we are alive.

Present *is* perfect.

conclusion: the legacy of connections

Perfectionists tend to value achievement over connection. But you're not just after perfection; you're after the *legacy* of perfection. Your pursuit of perfection is a shot at immortality. With legacy at stake, you have no time to waste, so doing takes precedence over being with others. Relating and companionship are often seen as a waste of time unless they are part of a networking effort. Some perfectionists are all business all the time: every handshake is an entry into a Rolodex, every name is a lead. Hard on yourself, you tend to hide from intimacy in fear that others will disapprove of your imperfections. Hard on others, you are at risk of alienating them with your criticisms. With time, the circle of connection shrinks.

You can correct the balance of doing and being, of distance and closeness, with the help of identification. After all, to identify is not only to forgive, but also to relate. As you take your time to learn to forgive, recognize that while a lack of forgiveness burns the bridges of connection, forgiveness rebuilds them.

pardon of acceptance

In closing the book, I want to leave you with three thoughts to meditate on. They are:

1. Accept all your movement as growth.

2. Stumble and try to regain the original balance.

3. Imperfection, like perfection, has no margin of error.

Be well! You know how.

references

Austin, J. 1999. *Zen and the Brain: Toward an Understanding of Meditation and Consciousness.* Cambridge, MA: First MIT Press.

Beck, A. T., A. Freeman, and D. D. Davis. 2004. *Cognitive Therapy of Personality Disorders.* New York: Guilford Press.

Blatt, S. 1995. The destructiveness of perfectionism. *The American Psychologist* 50(12): 1003-1020.

Callender, C., and R. Edney. 2005. *Introducing Time.* Cambridge, UK: Icon Books, Inc.

Chopra, D. 1993. *Ageless Body, Timeless Mind: The Quantum Alternative to Growing Old.* New York: Harmony Books.

CNN. 2009. German billionaire kills self, family says. Press release, January 6. www.cnn.com/2009/WORLD/europe/01/06/germany. billionaire/index.html.

De Bono, E. 1990. *Lateral Thinking: Creativity Step by Step.* New York: Harper & Row.

Flett, G. L., and P. L. Hewitt. 2002. *Perfectionism: Theory, Research, and Treatment.* Washington, DC: American Psychological Association.

Golomb, E. 1995. *Trapped in the Mirror: The Adult Children of Narcissists in Their Struggle for Self.* New York: Quill/William Morrow & Co.

Halberstam, D. 1965. *The Making of a Quagmire: An Uncompromising Account of Our Precarious Commitment in South Vietnam.* New York: Random House.

Harp, D. 1999. *The Three Minute Meditator.* New York: MJF Books.

Heine, S., and D. S. Wright, eds. 2000. *The Koan: Texts and Contexts in Zen Buddhism.* New York: Oxford University Press, USA.

Herrigel, E. 1953. *Zen in the Art of Archery.* New York: Pantheon Books.

Hurka, T. 1993. *Perfectionism*. New York: Oxford University Press, USA.

Jackson, S., and M. Czikszentmihalyi. 1999. *Flow in Sports: The Keys to Optimal Experiences and Performances*. Champaign, IL: Human Kinetics.

Kabat-Zinn, J. 1994. *Wherever You Go, There You Are: Mindfulness Meditation in Everyday Life*. New York: Hyperion.

Kim, Hee-Jin. 2000. Dogen Kigen: Mystical realist. In *The Koan: Texts and Contexts in Zen Buddhism*, eds. S. Heine and D. Wright. New York: Oxford University Press, USA.

Langer, E. J. 1989. *Mindfulness*. New York: Perseus Books.

Mamardashvilli, M. 2000. *Aesthetics of Cognition*. Moscow, Russia: Moscow Institute of Political Research.

Maxmen, J. S., and N. Ward. 1995. *Essential Psychopathology and Its Treatment*. New York: W.W. Norton.

Millon, T., and R. Davis. 2000. *Personality Disorders in Modern Life*. New York: Wiley.

New York Times. 1927. Isadora Duncan, dragged by scarf from auto, killed. September 15. http://select.nytimes.com/gst/abstract.html?res=F30C10F9355F17738DDDAC0994D1405B878EF1D3&scp=1&sq=Isadora%20Duncan,%20dragged%20by%20scarf%20from%20auto&st=cse

Orwell, G. 1949. *Nineteen Eighty-Four*. New York: Harcourt Brace Jovanovich, Inc.

Ouspensky, P. D. 2001. *In Search of the Miraculous: Fragments of an Unknown Teaching*. New York: Mariner Books.

Pfohl, B., and N. Blum. 1991. Obsessive-compulsive personality disorder: A review of available data and recommendations for DSM-IV. *Journal of Personality Disorders* 5:363–375.

Pope, A. 2006. *The Major Works: Oxford World's Classics*. New York: Oxford University Press, USA.

Rilke, R. M. 1986. *Letters to a Young Poet*. Trans. and foreword by Stephen Mitchell. New York: First Vintage Books Edition.

Radhakrishnan, S., and C. A. Moore. 1957. *A Source Book in Indian Philosophy*. Princeton, NJ: Princeton University Press.

Shapiro, D. 1981. *Autonomy and Rigid Character*. New York: Basic Books.

Somov, P. G. 2000. Time perception as a measure of pain intensity and pain type. *Journal of Back & Musculoskeletal Rehabilitation* 14(3): 111–121.

Somov, P. G., and M. J. Somova. 2003. *Recovery Equation: Motivational Enhancement, Choice Awareness, Use Prevention: An Innovative Clinical Curriculum for Substance-Use Treatment*. New York: Imprint Books.

Tart, C. 1994. *Living the Mindful Life: A Handbook for Living in the Present Moment*. Boston, MA: Shambhala Publications.

Wilber, K. 1998. *The Essential Ken Wilber: An Introductory Reader*. Boston, MA: Shambhala Publications.

Yerkes, R. M. and J. D. Dodson. 1908. The relation of strength of stimulus to rapidity of habit-formation. *Journal of Comparitive Neurology and Psychology* 18: 459–482.

Pavel Somov, Ph.D., is a licensed psychologist in private practice in Pittsburgh, PA. After serving in the Soviet military and completing his undergraduate degree at Moscow State Pedagogical University, he immigrated to the United States to pursue a career in psychology. He received his doctorate from State University of New York at Buffalo. Somov is author of *Eating the Moment*.

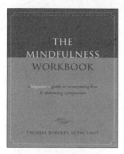
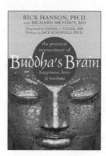

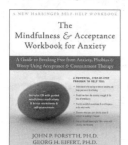